I QUIT!

THE LIFE-AFFIRMING
JOY OF GIVING UP

I QUIT!

THE LIFE-AFFIRMING
JOY OF GIVING UP

BY

COONOOR BEHAL

NEW DEGREE PRESS

COPYRIGHT © 2021 COONOOR BEHAL

I QUIT!

The Life-Affirming Joy of Giving Up

ISBN   978-1-63676-948-6   *Paperback*

           978-1-63730-014-5   *Kindle Ebook*

           978-1-63730-116-6   *Ebook*

To all the happy, brave quitters out there; past, present, and future.

NOT dedicated to the status quo or the thinking it inspires.

And to all my wiseass friends who said if I finished this book, I'd be a hypocrite. Love you, you goofs.

Contents

———

Introduction

As an innovation and creativity consultant, I one thousand percent believe this quote to be true. I spend my days working with clients who want to change their mindsets, skills, behaviors, organizational systems, and cultures to better embrace change.

My journey to doing the work that I do is inextricably tied to my love for quitting and quitting stories. I counsel clients on pivoting (thinking, products, services, and more), but what is the biggest pivot you can make? A hard quit. A "No more, thanks." "Never again." "Been there, done that." I am giddy every time I can help a client get to the mindset of "Who cares if that's how we've always done it? That's not how we are going to do it anymore."

To quit is to change your mind. Quitting is progress toward the new.

Quitting stories were a part of me starting my business. During the ritualistic "let's compare career trajectories" small talk that is endemic to Washington, DC—where I lived at the time—I vividly recall stopping people every time they said something along the lines of "Oh, and then I transitioned out of that job and then I..." or "Then I left that city and..." I would say, "Whoa wait, back up! Tell me more about why you left that job/city?" I found that this was a way to get to know someone at a deeper level than their resume or chronological history. I heard stories about people leaving jobs because they did not feel respected, they needed more money, or due to family pressure. I heard stories of uprooting lives and leaving cities for reasons big and small. By asking people "Why?" I learned a lot about their values, belief systems, and what was important to them. I learned about what they were willing to endure or not put up with. From these stories, as well as my own quitting experiences, I began to view quitting as not something "losers" do or as "giving up," but as making a life choice and making *progress*.

I may love a good quitting story now (enough to fill an entire book with them), but I wasn't' always so quick to change or question things, myself.

I was one of those (probably irritating) "achievers" growing up. I wasn't simply a part of every club but the leader/president of it. I was class president and then student council president, homecoming queen, choral leader, lead in the senior musical… you get it. You are probably nauseated by it, and I don't blame you. My beloved high school guidance counselor, Mr. Cusick, once half-jokingly said I reminded him of Tracey Flick, the devastatingly aspirational high school student

Reese Witherspoon played in the movie *Election*. Yeah, I got the reference; on top of everything, this super-achiever also had a part-time job at Hollywood Video. I was in on the joke. Mr. Cusick was my high school tennis coach for a bit too. I wasn't even good at tennis, but I never quit playing.

Bottom line, I was a joiner. A do-er. Someone whose word mattered. I took my commitments seriously. I wasn't a quitter.

It's what we all learn: you can't be a quitter *and* a high achiever.

But in college, I quit something that would impact the rest of my life.

I grew up a comedy nerd, so when I got to college in New York City, I immediately applied for internships available at all of the late-night talk shows. My sophomore year, I got an internship at *Late Night with Conan O'Brien*! It was at *Late Night* where an older intern suggested that I take an improv class at the theatre she attended. "I think you're really funny. I think you'd like it," she said. Ever susceptible to flattery and believing what others saw in me, I signed up for an eight-week improv class.

I went to the first class and was pretty immediately uncomfortable. I remember doing a two-person scene with a young, offbeat high school kid; he initiated a scene with me by clucking like a chicken and flapping his arms. I froze. I was uncomfortable. I had no idea how to respond, despite the instructor's gentle prodding that any response was a good one. After a long, awkward silence while the whole class waited for me to do something, anything, I blurted out, "I'm going to eat you!" to my classmate, the chicken. I was bad at improv. Not because of what I said, but because of how long it took me to unfreeze in the face of ambiguity. I left that first class and never went back. I quit improv.

I regretted it immediately and for years afterward. I continuously wondered, "What if I hadn't quit? Would I have loved it? Would I be writing for a comedy show right now?" With the benefit of growing up, gaining hindsight, and—mainly—becoming less of an annoying, achieving perfectionist, I realized a few things about this "Tracey Flick" I was at age twenty:

1. I was used to being good at things.
2. I was used to being good at things because I was carefully selecting and opting-in to only things in which I knew I had a good chance of success. I rarely truly challenged myself.
3. I wasn't good at improv.
4. No one is good at improv right away! Or even for, like, the first five years after they start doing it!
5. I wondered what would have happened if I'd just gone back to the next week's class. I now know that I would have learned that no one is good at improv at the start.
6. I was afraid of learning I was bad at something that might have been important to my career aspirations at the time. Being bad at something wasn't fun for me. So, I just chose not to learn anything about it or about myself at all.
7. I still wanted to do improv.

This was a *bad* quit. It permitted me to stay in my comfort zone, achieving for the sake of achieving, and put off the big life decisions that would allow me to curate my life (those came later and are referenced below).

After eight years of regret, wondering "what if?" and with the benefit of some *good* quits during those years, I wanted to get the monkey off my back. I signed up for an improv class. I remember sitting in a circle with the other students at the very first class, each of us awkwardly perched in the brightly colored, child-size chairs in the rented preschool classroom. The teacher, six years younger than me, asked us all to introduce ourselves and say why we signed up for the class. When my turn came, I said I had signed up "to settle an old, emotional score with myself."

This was the start of a now ten-year-long devotion to long-form improv comedy. I loved it. I even loved it when I was bad at it, which was and remains often. I not only went back to that same theatre in New York and took that class, but I also took all the others they offered. Improv is even a big part of my innovation and creativity work now. I "un-did" this bad quit.

The reason I share this example of a bad quit to introduce a book about stories of people who *don't* regret quitting things in their lives is because even though I quit improv on my first try, I learned so much about myself in processing why I quit and why I regretted this decision so deeply.

What we quit is a reflection of ourselves. The reasons *why* we quit teach us a lot about who we are and who we want to become.

So why do we resist quitting–change and progress–so much in our lives?

We all were raised to view quitting as a failure of character. Whether it was from youth sports, not being allowed to quit piano lessons, or even eyebrows raising when you announced you were not, in fact, going to continue with your economics major when you were just two classes away from getting it, we all "know" that quitting is bad.

Our society has a lot to say about quitting. Just Google "quitting quotes" and oh my god, you will soon learn just how oppressive it is out there for all of us. This is just a sampling:

- "Pain is temporary. Quitting lasts forever," (Lance Armstrong. Are you really going to take quitting advice from an infamous cheater?)
- "If you quit once, it becomes a habit. Never quit." (Michael Jordan)
- "It's always too soon to quit." (Vincent Norman Peale)
- "Age wrinkles the body; quitting wrinkles the soul." (Douglas MacArthur)
- "Quitting is the easiest thing to do." (Robert Kiyosaki)

And then there's the granddaddy of them all: "Quitters never win, and winners never quit" by Napoleon Hill. Countless people, especially Americans, have been brought up with this cross-stitch-on-a-pillow worthy philosophy from this self-help author who was once also deemed "The most famous con man you've probably never heard of."[1] From the time we are children, we are inculcated into a culture that equates

---

1   Matt Novak, "The Untold Story of Napoleon Hill, The Greatest Self-Help Scammer of All Time," *Gizmodo*, December 6, 2016.

reliability, character, commitment, and self-respect with not quitting.

Not quitting doesn't imply there is anything in its place. It's just the absence of something, the absence of a choice, really. We've grown up in a world that glorifies "sticking it out" as a path to success or to (equally undefined) "winning."

If there is one thing that I've learned in writing this book and interviewing people about their quitting stories, it's that the decision to quit and the reasons to do it are 100 percent individual and personal.

Case in point: I recently was interviewed about this book for a podcast, and I shared this formative story of mine about quitting improv and regretting it. Turns out, the host had also quit improv in college! But for her, it was one of the best decisions she ever made. "[Quitting improv] was the right thing for me. It was horrible. I fucking hated it. And it's part of what made me embrace that I was meant to be a lawyer." She never looked back, and she had zero regrets. We both quit the exact same thing at the same time in our lives and came to entirely different conclusions about it. Mine was a bad quit, hers was one of the best quits of her life.

This is why this book isn't about *how* to quit… or even about what constitutes a "good" or "bad" quit. There is no instruction manual for quitting.

Quitting is a means to learn about ourselves, to learn about our tradeoffs and our values. And as the stories in this book show, quitting can be a great way to actually *live* your values.

Even though quitting improv revealed things about myself I didn't particularly like, learning that the hard way allowed me to become more of a risk-taker, more of a "let's try it, why the hell not?" kind of person instead of a perfectionist intent on doing the "right" thing. In so many ways, personal and professional, quitting improv became the primordial ooze against which I built my life in a very different way than that twenty-year-old Tracey Flick type might have done. While this book focuses on stories about no-regrets quitting, even the "bad" quits can teach you a lot about yourself.

Society and its pithy sayings have tricked us into believing that quitting something or making a big decision is a risk. But who is to say that "sticking it out" in that job, relationship, or that identity isn't riskier than quitting? We all know the phrase, "Damned if you do, damned if you don't." Why can't we look at quitting similarly and think "It's a risk if you do, it's a risk if you don't?" Why is stasis and living life with inertia seen as less risky than decisive change and forward momentum?

Quitting is a choice. But so is *not* quitting.

Despite being a born achiever and completionist, I think I always had a bit of quitter in me. I remember visiting home during college and my dad, a lifelong doctor who had to choose his career when he was in eighth grade, called me into his den for a "talk." He basically advised me to "find a good job with a good company and stay there forever." I remember laughing out loud and without even thinking, replying, "That's not how the world works anymore, Dad." Despite not having had a career yet and having zero knowledge about global and domestic economic policies playing out at the time, I knew that the career loyalty and commitment of my parents' generation was a thing of the past. My generation saw parents stay in horrible marriages "for the kids" when the kids might have been better off with happily divorced parents. My generation grew up with stories of our elders dropping dead the day after they retired from a lifelong job they hated. In that moment in my dad's den, I think I knew that my life was going to have to include a lot of pivoting, reinvention, and starting over. In essence, I'd do a lot of quitting.

I've kept a mental tally of my "Quitting Inventory" over the years, ever since the bad improv quit. I have "good" quit:

- Three careers
- Two full-time jobs
- Two friendships (one of which I have since un-quit)
- Two romantic relationships
- One marriage
- Six cities

I encourage you to do your own "Quitting Inventory." Even if you think you haven't quit anything, you may be surprised by what a quick re-examination of your life choices yields.

Your Quitting Inventory is a surface-level start. Asking "why" you quit those things will get to the heart of who you are, what you value, and what you want out of life.

I asked every person I spoke to for this book to complete the following sentence: "I wasn't willing to put up with _____."

For me, my quits, good and bad, can be summed up as follows:

I wasn't willing to put up with...

- Sexual harassment and not feeling safe in the workplace.
- Learning that I might be bad at something I loved (ahem, improv).
- Risking my college GPA.
- Being treated with complacency and negligence.
- Other people toying with my livelihood.
- Letting a man make me feel insecure about myself.
- Not working in a meritocracy.
- Living in a one-industry town.
- Needing to spend more time navigating bureaucracy and office politics than actually doing work.
- The expectation that I stay polite and quiet in the face of selfishness and racism.

I share many of these personal reflections in the book. This list of things I wasn't willing to put up with is essentially a list of my life's biggest choices, my biggest swings for the fences. This list is a life of values and tradeoffs of which I am incredibly proud. Every single one of them propelled me on to a better version of myself and nudged me closer to actually finding what I wanted from life, love, and labor. It's a list of active choices of being an active participant in my life. One thing I know for sure from this list is that my life will not be one lived based on inertia.

One of the lovely people who shared their story for this book said this about summoning the courage to quit: "When we have very few examples of what the alternative would look like, it often seems safer to just stick with the status quo."

This is why I chose to use stories from everyday people to inspire and motivate us to rethink and destigmatize quitting. These give numerous examples of the alternative to toeing the line, living your life for other people, and being stuck because you are "sticking it out."

The stories in this book go beyond just their "I Quit _____" titles. You'll encounter themes and discussions around topics that span more than what the storytellers quit, including:

- Quitting due to gained knowledge
- Quitting to benefit others
- Quitting as an act of privilege
- Quitting things at which you excel
- Quitting as a singular act versus an ongoing choice to be made
- Quitting's intersections with family, class, race, and culture

My hope is that this book will be a small contribution to changing the stigma around quitting and quitters and will start to normalize quitting as a sign of self-awareness, self-worth, courage, and progress. I hope reading this book makes you entirely rethink how you view quitting and quitters. It will encourage you to reexamine your own quitting experiences through a new paradigm. It may even inspire you to make that next big, positive change for yourself.

So, instead of letting all those toxic quitting aphorisms seep into your psyche and rule how you live your life, allow me to offer you a much better "pillow worthy" statement:

"Of all the stratagems, to know when to quit is the best."

CHINESE PROVERB

And if you decide to quit this book before finishing it, you will have done me the honor of proving the inspiration within these pages. Thank you!

Names and other factual details have been changed, generalized, or omitted in some chapters to protect the privacy of those who shared their stories.

QUITTING HABITS

I Quit Drinking Soda

Jeff is the doting father of a little girl, but he didn't really care for his own childhood.

"There was nothing bad about it. I didn't hate it. I just felt like, 'thank God I grew up. Thank God I became an adult so I could become this different person. Childhood wasn't the defining time of my life.'"

Damn you, Jeff, and all the money you are probably saving on therapy.

Jeff's quitting origin story is unique because of this outlook. Many people trace their initial stigmas around quitting to their childhood years and how they were (or weren't) raised. But for Jeff, childhood is and was just one of many things in life that should be impermanent.

"I think it's awesome to change and evolve. To get past things is good. And part of that is quitting."

He especially felt this right to leave things behind around age thirty, when he began to realize that many of his friendships were on life support, sustained only by a sense of nostalgia.

"I was hanging on to these friendships just because they'd always been there. Maybe it has to do with laziness. But I realized who was and who wasn't adding value to my life. I told myself, 'Fuck that, I'm not lazy, I'm going to put in whatever work is needed to make my life better without carrying that shitty weight on my shoulders.'"

Jeff's willingness to "do the work" was pivotal to his most meaningful quitting story: he quit drinking soda.

His addiction to soda, ironically enough, does begin in what Jeff considers to be a mere blip in his life: his childhood. The fridge in the house he grew up in was always the envy of every other boy in the neighborhood; it groaned with the weight of all the Coke, Sprite, and Dr. Pepper (just to name a few) two liters filling it.

"My mom did all the grocery shopping, and I guess it just never occurred to her that it was bad for us," he says, still baffled. Jeff constantly had cavities. Maybe all that money saved on therapy was just front-loaded to the dentist.

"Because I now know the cause of them, I know that I grew up addicted to soda. I was drinking it all the time. It was like most people drink water. Getting something to eat? Get a Coke. It was normal. Every fucking meal there was soda."

Jeff isn't one hundred percent certain if he had an addiction or a habit. This line can be fine for many people.

"I honestly can't tell. It felt like both. I'm sure it was both. I know it was at least partially an addiction because I tried quitting it several different times."

Jeff told me it was likely more than a habit because of all the trouble he put himself through to kick it. The constant presence of soda in his life and the ensuing struggles he went through to quit elevated it to an addiction.

The first time he tried to quit soda was right after he broke up with a serious girlfriend. He had moved to Kansas City, Missouri, for her in his early thirties. While he was there, playing "SO" to an incredibly busy veterinary student, working his job remotely, and having a hard time meeting people, going out to grab something to eat was a reason to get out of the house and engage with his new world.

"I'd leave the house every day to get lunch... and there'd always be a Coke with it. Even if I found someone to go to a bar with, I'd always get a Captain and... wait for it...Coke! It was always present in my life, every day. I think I got a soda every single weekday for three years."

After the breakup, he moved in with a friend two hours away. "Getting hot," as Jeff puts it, became the priority.

"It was that whole bounce back body thing," he laughs. "I had a belly going. It was the first time I really considered what drinking soda was doing to my body. Now I'm single, I need to look hot right?" he laughs.

Like a lot of first-time quitters of addictions and habits, Jeff tried to quit cold turkey. I imagine he assumed it would be as simple as "quitting" childhood…it's just something that happens, out of which you evolve.

"It never occurred to me to think about *how* to quit. I just decided to stop. And that totally failed. I'd go a week without it and then think 'Oh I miss it; I'm just going to have one.' The next thing you know, you're just drinking it again like before."

Jeff moved back to the East Coast with his habit intact. He made another feeble attempt at quitting by cutting out soda *except* for the Captain and Cokes he liked so much when he was going out and enjoying the single life.

"Analyzing what's going on in your brain is weird. It was like my brain was telling me that I need to have soda and, if I don't have soda, there's a problem. It led me to come up with these weird excuses like, 'Oh, if there's alcohol mixed in, then it's fine.' This was total bullshit, of course."

Even when soda wasn't within his or a bartender's reach, Jeff had it on the brain. He'd sit at his desk at work, and by 10 a.m. he'd already be thinking about lunch and a deliciously sweet can of Dr. Pepper.

Jeff even altered his other life preferences to fit his soda addiction. He knew that all the fast-food chains were the same—"all the same horrible crap"—but he'd tell himself that Burger King was a lot better and pretend it tasted better. There was an ulterior motive, of course: Burger King was the only one of the chains that carried his soda of choice.

His tone resembles that of a beyond his prime rock star thinking back to those good old days, "That was my moment. I'd go to Burger King, get my little meal and the biggest soda I could, and just sit in my car, listen to talk radio, and just guzzle. And I'd be so happy." He shakes his head in disbelief at how elated he was in those moments.

Jeff stops himself when he starts to say those moments were the best part of his day, because he feels it would be insulting to the woman he was dating at the time and who is now his wife. Jeff attempted another quit while they were dating because of a predictable need for more dental work: two root canals in two years.

"I was able to cut out the soda for the couple of weeks after each one, so the dentist could assess the situation. Sometimes I'd be able to stretch it to a month at a time, but with cheat weekends built in. I was always talking about it with her. I'm sure I sounded like a child."

But it wasn't thinking of his childhood that finally got him to quit soda; it was thinking of Kiki's, his three-year-old daughter. He remembers a specific moment when he, his wife, and Kiki were all sitting down to dinner. He was sitting across from Kiki, unscrewing a bottle of soda, ready to chug it. He suddenly felt self-conscious, exposed, and worried.

"Do I want her to have this visual and think that this is just a normal thing to do? That she could have this problem? Soda is disgusting and no one should drink it. If I mean it when I say that I attribute my problem to that refrigerator door with all those two-liter bottles in my childhood, if I mean it when I trace my psychology around soda back to that, then I need to remove that from her life."

I'm both so impressed and in awe of Jeff that his daughter could be such a motivator for him to quit something that was so obviously ingrained in his psychology; it also makes me a touch wistful and jealous. I wish my own father had been able to quit smoking when I was a kid... I wish I could remember even seeing him attempt to do so.

I envy Kiki because her dad thinks she's worth the hard work to quit his habit. I've always had a strong sense of self-worth. I knew I was worth my dad trying to quit smoking. I was worth more than him just being forced to smoke in the garage instead of the house after I was diagnosed with asthma. My entire life, I've struggled with what to take away from this experience. Was addiction that hard to beat? Or was my dad not strong enough? What it felt like, then and feels like now, is that I wasn't worth the effort.

My dad quitting cold turkey would have been unthinkable. The cold turkey method was, again, not in the cards for Jeff either.

"In 2019, I did pretty well. I cut back on the cheat weekends. But I did slip up every once in a while."

This time, the siren call came from new, "craft" made sodas that boasted "natural" and "organic" ingredients like pure sugar cane on the label. Jeff was like a crack addict who had discovered cocaine.

"I told myself, 'Oh wow, well, this has got to be healthier for me.'" He knew what he was doing; he knew he was inventing excuses to drink it simply because it was delicious and he wanted it. He did go cold turkey on one thing, though. "I stopped drinking soda when Kiki was around. I'd always drink it by myself."

I think about my dad, shivering in the garage in the winter, smoking by himself.

2019 was about Jeff reducing and limiting soda. He'd had the motivation in Kiki, but he didn't have the training or the habits formed yet. 2019's practice run gave him that. As 2020 approached, he decided to get more serious and Q.U.I.T.

"It was a secret New Year's resolution to me. I don't think I even told my wife about it. It wasn't for anybody but me at this point. I'd already gone through the cheat weekends and the other bullshit. It wasn't anyone else's problem anymore."

Jeff tells me his quitting story in August 2020. Has he "evolved" out of quitting soda?

"Nothing. Not one drink of soda."

I want to high-five him! Give him a chest bump! Something to show how proud and happy I am for him. Words don't seem like they're enough.

He still has moments of desire, but instead of them getting the better of him, he can now laugh about them.

"This year, Dr. Pepper dropped a new flavor, and I was like 'Really? *Now*? Where was this last year?' It's actually funny to me, and I can laugh at it and really think 'Who cares?' I understand that this mission I'm on is bigger and more important than knowing how this new flavor tastes."

I may not have a "make the next generation of my bloodline better" motivation like Jeff does, but deciding not to care what something tastes like is super familiar to me. I have a big sweet tooth; I grew up hearing my grandmother and mother say that dessert goes to its own compartment in the stomach. The idea was there is always room for dessert, no matter how much non-dessert you might have eaten before! I totally still subscribe to this; dessert is about flavor sensation in your mouth, not about filling your belly. People who refuse dessert because they "aren't hungry" are weirdos who shouldn't be trusted. I, on the other hand, in the throes of good judgment, once yelled, "I feel like a fucking sultan!" as I ate an entire container of cake frosting with a spoon. When I try to cut back on sweets for health reasons or in an effort to just eat like a goddamned adult, I try to ask myself a question that reminds me of Jeff not caring what the new Dr. Pepper flavor tastes like: "Coonoor, do you already know what that cookie/chocolate cake/muffin/brownie/entire package of double dark chocolate Milanos tastes like?" If I take a beat and ask myself this before grabbing the sweet treat, the answer 99 percent of the time is yes. *Yes*, I know what that is going to taste like: "Do I want it, anyway?"

I won't comment on how this strategy is working for me, but Jeff points to quitting soda as something that's helped him stave off the worst "Dad bod."

"I think back to my first motivation to quit, which was physique and looks, and because I quit soda, I definitely eat a lot less other sugar. The stash of Starburst I used to keep at my desk has disappeared. I'm definitely in better shape physically and mentally than if I hadn't stopped drinking soda."

If there is any downside to Jeff conquering his addiction, it's the looming threat of becoming an annoying "Don't you know" jerk.

"I've always hated those people who learn something new and then start instructing you about it like they've been doing it their entire lives. I caught myself once beginning to do that and telling a coworker who would go to McDonald's a lot something like, 'Oh, you know the sodas aren't great for you, right?' And I was like, 'Oh my god, Jeff, *stop*. Fuck you, Jeff, you've been drinking soda for forty-two years. She's on her own path, don't pretend you are better than her.'"

I'm grateful Jeff's fear of becoming "that" jerk didn't prevent him from telling his quitting story.

"I do worry that by telling people about it, I'll somehow jinx it. Or that I should wait until it's been a full year before I go brag about it like I've actually done something."

Here, Jeff is displaying a quality I think is common in successful quitters: humility. To quit something is to admit you made a poor decision at one point or that the decision you previously made is no longer working for you. To admit to either of these, vulnerability is essential.

Jeff does wish he had stopped drinking soda much earlier. But he's self-compassionate about it.

"I honestly don't know when it would have happened before. I guess it wouldn't have happened because I was motivated by another person. I do wish I would have found that internal motivation, but what worked, worked."

I encourage him not to be too hard on himself, Kiki's lucky her dad did something that hard for her.

"I couldn't be prouder of doing what I've done," he says. "It was hard as hell, and it was years and years in the making."

Quitting soda has also given Jeff more empathy for others who are "in recovery."

"I feel like I have this understanding now for people who have recovered from alcoholism. I get the need to not be around certain triggers or make choices about what and who you'll have in your environment. To think of some asshole saying to someone 'Oh, just have one,' to someone like me…what might be jokey to you could be a life-changing moment for me that throws me off this path I'm happy to be on."

* * *

What if you hadn't quit?

"If I hadn't quit drinking soda, I would feel bad about myself. Even before I decided to stop drinking in front of Kiki, I would feel gross when I drank it. I would definitely be less healthy."

What's the story you tell yourself about this quitting experience?

"Right now, I feel so relaxed about it. For about ten years, it was a major topic in my life that mattered all the time. I was constantly thinking about it and talking about it. This year, I can finally just not think about it, and that's so relaxing."

What tradeoffs did you accept by quitting?

"The number one trade I've made by quitting soda is the choice in where I'll go to eat. I won't even go to a fast-food chain anymore because it was such a habit to drink soda at those places that I'm afraid my brain will go on autopilot from years of training and order a soda."

What does this quitting story say about you?

"Quitting soda says that I mean it when I say I care about Kiki and about being a dad. I really mean if something is going to be bad for her, I'm willing to make it a priority to remove it from her life. I'm proud of the fact that it shows I'm willing to make sacrifices for her."

"It's very important to me that one can put aside things from childhood and be an adult. It shows that I can change, and that's very, very important to me. I love growing, learning, and changing. You have to be the type of person that's willing to say 'Something I'm doing isn't good enough right now, and I'm willing to change and grow.'"

"I wasn't willing to put up with _____."

"I wasn't willing to put up with the idea that my habits could have a negative impact on my daughter's health."

I Quit Heroin

Trigger warning: drug addiction

Younas didn't step in to his first Narcotics Anonymous (NA) meeting until he'd already been clean for a few years. Growing up in Pakistan in the 2000s, he didn't have easy access to methadone clinics, reputable NA programs, or rehab centers when he was trying to quit; he had quit cold turkey, relying on only willpower and family support.

So, it's understandable that Younas immediately rejected one of NAs core principles: that everyone who has quit drugs is in a constant state of recovery. At that first meeting, he had been corrected when he had introduced himself as "recovered" from his years-long heroin addiction.

Past tense. Done. He wasn't quitt_ing_. He _had_ quit.

If you have stereotypes about heroin addicts, I guarantee you Younas doesn't fit them. My own stereotypes of heroin users and addicts are definitely informed by my upbringing in rural Ohio and my present home in the Pacific Northwest.

Heroin has always seemed to me a *white* person's problem, facilitated in no small part by the prejudice in medicine that means people of color's pain is not to be believed and therefore not treated as seriously as the pain of white people. I've experienced this myself, having gone to an emergency room away from home with what turned out to be a herniated disc in my neck and a pinched nerve that rendered my left arm useless. The pain was excruciating. It brought tears to my eyes that spinal fractures years prior had not; I learned later that many liken the pain of a cervical herniated disc to that of childbirth. During intake at the ER, the nurse repeatedly downgraded my description of my pain levels. I'd tell her something was an 8 out of 10, she'd say "Okay, I'll jot that down as a 6." The doctor ultimately gave me only enough painkillers for the cross-country flight home; when I got back, I was stuck and on my own.

I had experienced firsthand one reason why painkiller-driven heroin dependence has mostly impacted white people: racism.

Not only is Younas not white, but he also had a pretty comfortable, stable upbringing. His parents were well-off upper-middle-class professionals, and he went to good private schools.

Younas also never needed to steal to support his habit. His mom helped him buy his heroin.

"When she found out I was using," he says, "she started giving me money, so I'd never have to steal. That was one good thing that happened—I never got in trouble for theft. It really saved my conscience."

His mother had lost her brother to addiction years before. Younas's uncle had been in and out of Pakistan's rehab centers. Younas feels this made her smart enough to know how to handle his battle.

"I was always a rebellious teenager and always loved saying 'Fuck you' to authority. I was always fighting my parents, the school, or something else."

He found like-minded friends from other schools on internet chat rooms. They would get together and do what any high school boys do: they started a rock band.

"We were all just trying to be musicians," he remembers innocently. "At some point, it started to turn into this fantasy of sex, drugs, and rock and roll."

That fantasy eventually turned into just doing drugs all the time, letting the sex and the rock and roll fall by the wayside.

"I think all of us boys were messed up in the same way," he says. "We'd always find something bad to do, whether it was getting into fights or doing something illegal. We were always actively seeking those things out."

Younas was just thirteen years old when he started using. His addiction escalated in the following years.

"By the time I got to the equivalent of eleventh grade, I was pretty far gone. I would skip school a lot. By this point, I had my own circles of even more extreme junkies. I'd skip out on my private school friends to hang out with them."

Even as he speaks about skipping school, you can tell Younas thinks highly of his—and all—education.

"I had been really involved in extracurriculars; it was a big part of my identity. I was a theatre person. I was captain of the basketball team, an all-star athlete...my education gave me a lot."

I imagine it pained him when he ultimately decided to quit school. His school noticed that he wasn't showing up or putting in any effort, so they put him in a remedial program. Younas tried that for a bit but eventually knew he "couldn't play this game at that time."

Quitting school, for Younas, was connected to the decision to quit heroin. At the time he decided to kick his addiction, Younas didn't know anyone else who was using as much as he was, as often as he was, for as long as he had been who hadn't died.

Younas clearly remembers the moment he decided to quit. He was seventeen and sitting in one of the remedial classes to which he had been demoted.

"I sat there thinking how unhappy I was about my life. I felt like a pariah. I had a vision sitting there of the life I would have, and it scared me to my core. I had a very clear vision of the two choices I had. I could either go down this same path and probably die like my uncle, or I could make a different decision and stay alive."

He got up and left his class, hailed a rickshaw, and went straight home.

"I went to my parents and I said I can't do this anymore; I need to leave school and I need support." It was a very emotional moment for everyone, especially for his mom.

"She had been on this journey with me," Younas explains. "At the beginning, she'd reacted like a lot of parents, throwing my drugs away when she found them. But eventually, she had given up and accepted that this was her son, and she started going about it in a smarter way, like giving me the money that helped me retain my moral compass. I was very emotional at this moment because I felt so guilty about what she'd done for me and how hard they had worked to give me the life that I had. It didn't feel fair for them to go through all of this."

Through all the emotion, he knew exactly how he was going to quit.

"I told my parents that I didn't want to be like my uncle. The system, the rehab clinics, had failed him. It was going to have to be purely on willpower and done at home. This was going to be my second chance at living and being alive."

A series of "mini" quits followed: He flushed every drug he had. He didn't leave his parents' house. He gave his parents his cell phone and told them to lock it up. He burned the diary in which he had written all of his dealers' contact information.

But Younas leaving school and cutting off contact with his friends didn't stop them from showing up at his house regularly, honking their car horns, and yelling outside his house. Locked inside of his bedroom, Younas never wavered.

The following months were a painful abyss for Younas as he went through withdrawal. His parents supervised and monitored him every step of the way.

"I would experience complete blackouts. There are whole months that I don't remember because of how severe the pain was. It's not just psychological, but you feel excruciating pain in your brain and in your bones, your entire skeleton." Heroin addiction can certainly kill. But so can withdrawal. In a way, Younas had cheated death twice.

Younas says the second chance at life he got himself defined how he chose to view the world afterward. He became all about doing good and understanding society at large. As is the case for many others, quitting gave Younas the confidence to build a life that he actually wanted.

"Going through the pain of withdrawal made me feel like I could do anything afterward."

He finished his school examinations with the help of private tutors. He then gave himself what he calls "the gift" of two years to figure out what he wanted to do. He spent that time becoming a communist, joining socialist organizations and study circles, and also doing a lot of street theatre for children in the suburbs of Lahore.

"I was also one of those annoying guys with an accent who called you up and tried to sell you DISH Network for a while," he laughs.

As he was shaping his future, Younas also tried to help his former addict friends. This was one thing his confidence couldn't change.

"I wasn't very successful, and I eventually stopped taking it personally. I tried, but some of them were too far gone. I felt guilty because I felt responsible for many of the people I had gotten hooked."

It was around this time that Younas tried out NA and decided it wasn't for him.

"I had already decided to stop letting my addiction define myself. 'So,' I thought, 'I've fixed myself, so now can I fix these people, right? What can I do for the larger society?'"

By the time he started business school, he was a self-identified Marxist. Pakistan was experiencing anti-dictatorship protests at the time and Younas was, of course, involved.

"I was reading business textbooks and learning Marxist and feminist philosophy during the day and getting tear gassed and fighting with the police at night."

Younas has the self-awareness and confidence that I see in a lot of quitters. Like many in this book, he has no regrets.

"It's made me the person I am today. If I could quit heroin and go through that withdrawal experience, I knew I could do anything. I can't imagine another way or path that would have led me to that realization."

Also, like many quitters, this self-love and confidence come *from* the quitting.

It's also given him incredible perspective, even when in the throes of life's most difficult challenges.

"I've hit lows since, including going through a divorce. My mother passed away just before the [coronavirus] pandemic began. And the pandemic itself has also brought on a lot of depression, anxiety, and negativity. But I always have that rock bottom to compare to it. No matter what, if I'm in a shitty place I can always say 'At least I'm not there. It can only be uphill from here.' It's a big deterrent because going back to that place still scares me."

It's all too easy for someone like me who has never suffered from addiction to think that not wanting to do heroin after so much pain and death would be obvious; that not wanting to return to it would be easy. But then I hear how Younas describes what he gave up, what the tradeoff he accepted was:

"Let's be honest, being high on heroin is the greatest feeling in the world. That's why it's so addictive. I know that I've given that feeling up, and I'll never be able to experience that again."

I don't think I can honestly say I've ever experienced something I would call the "greatest feeling in the world," and I've lived an incredibly fortunate life. But in my own simpleton way, I try to think about my small comparisons. If I chose to never taste chocolate mousse on my tongue again, or to never feel the silky softness of my dog's fur in my face, or if I chose to never curl up with a good book and a glass of wine again, or to never float in the ocean again... I would be giving up a part of me, and I would be unrecognizable to myself.

To me, Younas's quitting heroin isn't just about him saving his life. It's about him getting a brand new one, but one that requires him to, on a daily basis, quite who he used to be.

I admire and respect Younas for sharing his story with me, not least because he is sharing it with another South Asian. A huge division exists between public and private life in our culture. You are not supposed to share private things with others outside of the family; you must "save face" at all costs and avoid the judgment of others. It's a cultural practice that, as you can imagine, doesn't always create the most forthcoming or honest interactions.

Younas's own honesty does get him into a wee bit of trouble on occasion, including in his work.

During his time doing street theatre, he actually had an interview for a school theatre director position. He was interviewed by his old high school principal.

"She instantly recognized me and asked me where I had disappeared to. My problem was that I was very honest at that moment, and I told her I became an addict and had quit school."

He didn't get the job. But Younas feels the honesty was worth the outcome.

"My friend was like, 'Why did you tell her that?' And I was like, 'Dude, she knew me as a child. I had to be honest!' I understood her perspective, I can put myself in her shoes."

Today, thirteen years after getting clean, he is an educator, creating curricula for a school in Lahore. He has served as a training manager at an organization that develops social change leaders. He and his old high school principal are colleagues now and take smoke breaks together during education conferences. He has no regrets about his honesty.

* * *

What tradeoffs did you accept by quitting?

"I gave up all my friends, who were the people I would do drugs with. A lot of them passed away. One of them passed away just last year. I've been to a lot of funerals. But I've gained the joy of having a second chance at being alive... I'd like to make something of it."

What does this quitting story say about you?

"It says that my life matters, whether I choose to believe it or not. It also says that I have something to fall back on when I'm at my lowest. I'll know I'm a level above my worst. That's something that gives me extra fuel and helps me pull myself out of situations. Even though I'm not always fine, I know I *will* be fine."

What makes you most proud of your quitting story?

"That I didn't let my addiction define me, ever. It's not my identity. Also, that I'm a functioning, productive member of society."

"My mom passed away happy with me. I was able to be there with her."

"I live with and take care of my dad now. I'm very happy to be counted on, be relied upon, and be responsible."

"I know a lot of people who had even more support than I did, and they didn't make it out. I'm proud that my quitting is something that only I can own, that this is something I have achieved. This is something that reminds me that I'm somewhat of a badass."

"I wasn't willing to put up with _____."

"I wasn't willing to put up with the life of a junkie."

I Quit a Life of Thugs and Drugs

Trigger warning: child sexual assault, sexual
assault, intergenerational trauma, systemic racism,
drug addiction, physical violence, and
suicidal ideation

Sometimes, quitting is the only way to save your life.

Leah and I are both from Ohio, but we were born into extraordinarily different circumstances. I grew up in an upper middle class, immigrant household. Tennis lessons. Math tutors. Bike rides with friends. While I was spending my time after school eating Milano cookies and watching *The Kids in the Hall,* three hours away and a few years earlier, Leah was meeting her family's expectations by doing drugs and committing crimes.

"I was born into a family where drugs and guns were the family business," she says "By the time I was five years old, I lost my mother, two brothers, and a sister to the violence of that world. I was a drug runner by the time I was seven, a full-blown addict by the time I was ten. I was fifteen when they taught me to steal cars. That was my contribution to the family business."

Leah used drugs as a coping mechanism. Uppers and downers to "deal with daily life," cocaine to "make the world seem like a good place," and heroin as "the escape."

Leah's mother was one hundred percent Blackfoot Native American. Her "hillbilly" father had won her in a poker game. Leah is very open about the privilege she had in this violent world because she could pass as white. Her privilege made the difference between life and death.

"I figured out very, very young that I'm white-passing, which gave me a higher level of accountability than my darker-skinned family. My father was the perpetrator that ultimately killed my darker-skinned mother, brothers, and sister. He made it pointedly clear that they were each just another dead Indian. But the white kid...you can't lose the white kid. People are going to ask questions, right?"

I grew up around mostly white kids in a racially segregated town. While I had a few experiences with racism directed at me and my brown skin, I never once felt physically unsafe because of it. Leah says her whiteness kept her comparably safer on Cleveland's racially divided streets.

"We didn't call them gangs at the time," she says, "but who 'your people' were determined where you could and couldn't be."

Her whiteness also allowed her to stay in school. One of the many times she was called into the principal's office was after she pulled a knife on a kid who tripped her in the hall. She says she knew she was going to be expelled as two large teachers dragged her to the principal's office. Another girl had been sent to juvenile detention just for getting in a shoving match the week before. Instead, Leah was greeted by a smile from the principal when she entered his office.

He said, "I'm going to send you home today. Be back on Monday and leave the blade at home. You hear me?"

Leah nodded, shocked.

"It was years later that I looked back," she says, "and I recognized that it was the perception that I was white. The other girl the week before couldn't even try to pass for white. Because I was a white kid, I wasn't held accountable. My best friend was Black and people were scared of her, this straight arrow; *I'm* the one they should have been scared of."

You might be surprised to learn that Leah, a self-described" "inner-city thug" who was in the family business of making money from crime, actually went to school at all. But the reason is so simple that she laughs when I, a drama and choir geek who occasionally smoked weed with the band kids, naively asked: "Why even bother with high school?"

"High school is a lucrative market for a drug dealer."

Leah's family didn't care about her education or how she did in school. She was there to sell drugs and scope out cars.

By the time Leah was fifteen and started stealing cars, she realized that being in your twenties was, well...*old* in her world. She'd seen a lot of people around her not make it past that age.

Leah may not have even made it that far if it wasn't for her high school guidance counselor.

"I came into school one day in the tenth grade and the guidance counselor asked me to come into her office. I didn't even know she had an office, the only office I was ever in was the principal's."

The guidance counselor sat Leah down and told her she was smart. Leah waited; usually, there was something that came after the "smart" like "ass" or "aleck."

"You scored better on your SATs than most of our graduating seniors," the guidance counselor said. "I want you to go into the advanced English class."

Leah came from a family that didn't value education. Her mom had a sixth-grade education, and her dad had an eighth-grade education. Her first thought was how accepting the guidance counselor's suggestion would ruin her reputation. She knew she'd get some verbal jabs or people would think she was playing a joke.

"Maybe it was divine intervention but, inside, I was actually excited to be challenged academically for a change. This was really the turning point for me."

Leah enrolled in the advanced English class.

"My response was to just shrink away in the class. But when that English teacher started to hold up my work in class as exemplary, I was like 'Wow, this is amazing!'" The same English teacher helped Leah with a big research project, essentially teaching her how to use the library in the process.

"We were supposed to report on another country," Leah remembers. "I had never even been out of my neighborhood! She spent hours with me in the library and taught me how to use the Dewey Decimal system. Through her, I learned that the library actually has this whole world to discover. And it opened up a whole new angle for me."

The guidance counselor soon started talking to Leah about going to college. She had already been considering if her best option was to try and rise to leader in the "thug world," or "just lay low, keep my head down, and try to make it out alive."

"When I looked at my life," she says, "I knew that going to college was my ticket out."

It would be great if going to college on a full scholarship was the end of Leah's quitting story… that through the power of education, she quit her life of thugs and drugs for good. But that isn't her story.

"The choices that came after deciding to go to college weren't easy," she says.

As the first person in her family—and possibly, her world—to go to college, she received a lot of criticism.

"I was taking a lot of pressure from home about 'getting too big for my britches' and 'who did I think I was' and other comments that were creating tension."

The treatment from her family wasn't as easy to brush off as the jabs her high school friends made when she enrolled in the advanced English class. It all contributed to Leah becoming suicidal. In her first semester of college, she even made a plan to end her life.

"There was a road with a tree," she describes, "and a ravine on the other side of the tree. Worst-case scenario, you miss the tree and you hit the ravine."

What stopped her from carrying out her plan was shockingly reasonable.

"The deterrent was I'd had enough pain in my life already. And if I don't die, it will hurt. A LOT," she laughs saying this, surely thinking about the absurdity of her choices back then.

Just as she did when deciding to go to college, Leah thought logically about her choices. She wanted to end her life to avoid more pain, but a failed attempt at ending her life could very well add to her existing pain.

Amidst relentless obstacles, her home life lured her back in.

Leah's dad, at a certain point, went to prison for a triple homicide. While he was in prison, he wrote Leah a letter saying how he was sorry, and he wanted things to be different. Leah realized she still wanted a dad in her life.

In her first year of college, her dad was released on what's called a "shock" probation after only eighteen months in prison. Leah assumes it was because of some blackmail or bribery.

"That's the way the system I knew worked."

When Leah was home for her first spring break, she went to see him. It was a huge mistake.

They got into an argument.

"He threw me into a table, which damaged my brain stem and my central nervous system. I probably would not have had significant damage except that I got on an airplane to go back to school in Nebraska and the pressure change was really bad for me. The moment the plane landed, I was put into an ambulance."

Leah spent two years as an inpatient and one year as an outpatient. She eventually gained most of her function back, but for a time she lost all ability from the neck down. She was deaf for the next nineteen years. She still has residual seizure disorder.

Of course, this interrupted her college plans in the very first year.

"I ended up back home and married my dealer."

Thus, began her re-entry to her old life of "thugs and drugs."

Growing up, Leah had experienced what she calls "the whole nine yards" of sexual abuse. She had been told she wouldn't be able to have children because of it. But she got pregnant. This motivated her to change.

"I quit all the drugs I was doing cold turkey. They said I'd be lucky if I carried the baby to full term given my history. They kept giving me these lists of things that could go wrong or be wrong with her," she says about her daughter. "My husband was in total agreement that I should be clean while we have this baby. But he wasn't thrilled I wanted to stay clean after our daughter was born."

Leah had a second child, a boy, seventeen months later. "Two miracles are enough for anybody."

Leah's husband began to physically abuse their son when he was nearly two years old. Leah wasn't going to have any of that.

"You can beat the hell out of me, but don't touch my kids. That was my mindset in that moment."

The perks of being married to her dealer diminished once Leah decided to stay clean. She no longer needed the drugs that helped her cope through the physical and sexual abuse.

"When those perks become detriments, you know it's time to quit." But Leah had no money of her own and nowhere to go.

She made a plan, this one very different from the plan she'd made in her first semester of college; this plan was to allow her to live. She began to siphon money off her husband's drug deals and eventually bought a car that was intentionally in only her name. As soon as she could, she got her kids and left.

Leah's life shifted and changed yet again, this time to that of a single mom on the run. She and her two small children were homeless and living in that car for the next seven months. Even after they found housing, she calls that period a time filled with "drop and runs" to try to stay ahead of the life that seemed to keep finding her.

"There were times I'd come home and say to my kids 'Okay, pack up one box each, we're leaving in two hours.' My daughter graduated from high school after attending fourteen schools. I carried a lot of mom guilt for that, but my kids are quick to tell me that they can make friends anywhere they are and are flexible people because of it."

She was in a constant state of fleeing her old life. It would sometimes catch up to her, and she'd start using again. The stakes were different now, though; she knew she had to quit.

"I've done a lot of leaving, a lot of letting go. The biggest challenge that I found was breaking those old habits. That's one of my frustrations. When I quit using and went to AA, at the time, they were like 'everybody relapses.' And I was like, 'I can't afford to relapse, I have two kids!'"

Leah eventually quit drugs cold turkey using the *Red Road to Wellbriety*, a book and method that encourages becoming "sober and well in the Native American cultural way."[2] After eleven years and eight colleges, she got her degree in psychology. Along the way, she worked for two years in Child Protective Services, but it soon chewed her up and she quit.

"I was a great CPS worker," she says, "because I could look at people in the eye and say, I did it so you can, too. But the system asks you to sign your name on paperwork and 'approve' things that made me not be able to sleep at night."

The last straw came when she was asked to sign off on placing a toddler who had physical evidence of sexual penetration into the home of a family member where a known, adolescent sexual offender was living. The logic, Leah says, was "she isn't' his victim."

"I refused to sign off. I could never have lived with myself."

She eventually got her dual master's in special education and general education to be a teacher and have a better work schedule to raise her kids. She quit that too, frustrated by the disconnect between the way children are taught versus the ways they need to learn.

When Leah thinks about all the things she left behind, most of which she was born into with no choice, she says she has lots of regrets.

---

2 *The Road to Wellbriety: In The Native American Way*'s Amazon page. Accessed February 23, 2021.

"Most of my regrets are things over which I have no control. They are the people I left behind because of the life I left behind. I'm a great rescuer, and that would be my downfall. I would love nothing more than to reach back and pull all those people forward with me, but that's not possible. You can't throw them a line unless they are willing to give up the struggle. I wish it had been easier," she laughs, having forgiven herself for failing.

Every failure is just another data point with which to make better decisions moving forward.

After learning new information about careers in CPS and in education and how they didn't match her values, Leah decided to pivot to entrepreneurship. But one thing about that world stumped her: marketing.

"I was having lunch with a good friend, and I told her that I just don't understand this marketing thing. She just looked at me and said, 'Leah, did you or did you not work the corner?' It was that moment that made me realize I'd been an entrepreneur my entire life; I was born into a family of entrepreneurs."

Leah is now a confident small business owner, helping educators and students nurture resilience with a focus on diversity, respect, and equity. She works in-depth with communities experiencing high poverty and trauma rates.

"I went into the work I do because I don't believe anyone should have to experience what I experienced. There are more people who have, though, than I care to think about.

I have the honor and the gift to share my story and use it in a constructive way."

When Leah thinks about what would have happened if she hadn't quit this old life, she's as blunt as you'd expect someone who gave herself the title "CEO & Badass Trainer."

"I wouldn't be alive. There are days when I wake up, and I'm now in my mid-fifties, and I think about how I thought I'd never have gotten this far," she marvels. "I do sometimes wonder what would have happened if, at certain crossroads, I went a different way. But, by and large, I'm happy with where I've been because it's made me who I am. And I like who I am. Did I get it all right? Hell no! Once I learned or had better, I did better."

To Leah, her quitting story is all about this course correction.

"We know about fighter pilots who spend seventy to ninety percent of their time in the cockpit course correcting. And so being 'right' really is about that course correction. And it gives me the permission to be wrong and to be humble about being wrong. I'm so grateful that this gives me the compassion for other people who are also course correcting in their own lives."

Just don't call her brave.

"Bravery and courage are when you see someone drowning in a river, and you *choose* to jump in and save them. What I did was survive. I'm hardwired as a survivor, so much so that my family knows my favorite mantra: 'I and the cockroaches will survive.'"

Quitting a life of thugs and drugs has, perhaps not surprisingly, defined who Leah is and her sense of self and purpose.

"I am a compassionate survivor who now has the opportunity to pay it forward and backward. People hurt me, and people have to help me heal. My belief system is such that, as I heal me, I heal for those that came before me and for those that come after."

* * *

When do you share this story with others?

"I share parts of it in every training and learning experience I offer. In diversity and equity work, layers compound from intersectionality, the impact of race, and the importance of allies. When talking about resilience and trauma, most of my work consists of helping people see what support is necessary, what else is possible, and why we don't ever write kids off."

What is the story you tell yourself about this quitting experience?

"It was my reset button. I was fortunate to have had a mother who loved me and told and showed me this, even though she was killed when I was three. I have always known I am loveable and that I am capable of love. This is the story of who I am and who I get to become because I took charge of the story line as soon as I had children. I watch my grandchildren now, who are clueless of that life, and I am proud of having broken that cycle."

What tradeoffs did you accept by quitting?

"I gave up my family and my roots. I gained my life, my future, and that of my family to the seventh generation."

What does this quitting story say about you?

"I am smart, strong, and fortunate."

What makes you most proud of your quitting story?

"My kids. They are absolutely amazing human beings and who they are is a direct result of who I am and where I've been. Those kids have what they have because I was hell bent on the cycle stopping with me."

What values does this quitting story say you have?

"I believe it reflects my three primary values: Life is sacred, treat it with love. At the core of all that is, there are relationships. We must honor and protect all that we have been given and teach others to do the same."

"I wasn't willing to put up with _____."

"In the moment, I wasn't willing to put up with my children being victimized. Ultimately, I was able to include myself. Now, I am not willing to put up with anything that doesn't support me, my community, and my world being the very best they can be."

QUITTING JOBS & CAREERS

I Quit Silicon Valley

Kathy still remembers the spittle on the Senior VP of Marketing's mouth. That's how close he was to her; how close he chose to bring his anger to her body that day twelve years ago. Her body that had fifteen years of success in the tech industry, twenty years as an improv comedy performer; her body that contained the brain that got her to be the Senior Director of Marketing Communications at the Silicon Valley company. Her body that also happened to be seven months pregnant.

It was Kathy's job to make sure that all the communications coming from the company sounded consistent and "not half-assed." As a professional marketer and longtime improviser, Kathy knows what it takes to be good at media relations: being quick on your feet, able to speak in sound bites, able to handle whatever gets thrown at you, and the art of the redirect.

"He wasn't good at any of this," she told me. She made the call to put someone else on the team in charge of talking to the press.

The VP called her into his office and made it clear that due to his title and because she reported to him, he should have the role. Kathy stood her ground. She explained to him that she felt they needed to do what was right for the company and put the better communicator on the job.

She couldn't believe what happened next.

"Here I am, pregnant, and he got in my face and got *this* close to me," she says, still in angry disbelief. "Spit started coming out of his mouth. It was like his head was going to explode, he was so angry. It wasn't justifiable; it was complete egocentricity."

Kathy recalls in that moment understanding that what she was witnessing was nothing but a temper tantrum.

"I'm working for somebody who doesn't care about doing right; this guy only cares about *being* right."

Having been around enough rage-filled men so frustrated by their own mediocrity that they behave like toddlers, I know this scene all too well. I've never found it cute when families refer to the husband/father as "another child" of whom the mom is taking care. Who wants to take care of an adult child? Hell, I don't even want to take care of a child-child. But Kathy was about to do just that. She was very conscious of her space being invaded by this ill-tempered man child.

"I honestly felt threatened, like my "mama bear" instincts were being triggered," she says.

Her fight or flight response was also being triggered. This was the wake-up call she'd been needing after years of being frustrated with the tech industry and "taking this kind of shit" more often than not.

"That was it," she says. "All of it just collided in that moment, and it was my 'aha' moment. I was like, I'm not doing this shit anymore."

Kathy chose flight.

She went to HR to report the incident, but they were not supportive and didn't have a lot of power.

"I remember thinking, thank God HR sucks so hard, you've just made my decision easier. It gave me tremendous clarity."

It was 2008. Kathy decided to leave her high-profile, lucrative tech career during the Great Recession to start her own storytelling consulting business, and just two months before her first child was born. That's just how fed up she was.

"It would have been crazier to stay," she says.

I know the feeling. I also quit a job at the end of 2008, my first after grad school. I quit because—after being sexually harassed my third month in—I couldn't trust the organization not to put me in similarly unsafe situations in the future. Even though I got the guy fired, he was allowed to go about his abusive ways for a decade before I ever got there. Removing one rotten apple from the tree doesn't get rid of the rot inside the trunk. I tried so hard to keep my head held high and go about my work professionally, but nothing would be the same for me after that; notably, none of my male superiors would ever be in a meeting or an office alone with me; they would always go into the hall and grab someone to "sit in," regardless of how irrelevant they were to the topic at hand. So many of my lines were crossed in that job that I quit "for" unemployment. I shudder to think that what I went through for only one and a half years before saying, "fuck this noise," Kathy experienced for fifteen years.

Sure enough, her decision wasn't rooted in just that one moment with Sir Spits-A-Lot. The frustration in Kathy had been building throughout her career. She had already been thinking of moving on. I find that women with values and standards for men's behavior aren't necessarily as "impulsive" as we may look to the outside observer.

"I didn't like the energy, the battles I had to fight," she says, exhaustion in her voice even years later. "As a woman in a very male-dominated space, I felt like not all of my gifts were being used. I was having to jump through hoops and make concessions in a world that doesn't value women and people of color, or at least in the way they should have. It's just a pattern: I'm putting in all this energy to try to make the workplace better for people, I'm trying to make it safer for women to speak up… but, honestly, I reached a point where I learned that it just doesn't matter."

Flashes of that first job again: our efforts to fix our places of employment are too often meaningless. I recall once I realized that I wasn't going to be able to have an impact on the people we were serving, I tried to have some impact on the organization itself. I actually put together a program of *free* (I'll say it again - *free*) professional development resources for junior staff; my leadership's response was, "We don't do that here."

I was a low-level employee at the time. But Kathy was a director. She had the position and the title behind her. Even then, she ran up against the limits of organizational change.

"The work got tokenized," she says, "and I no longer felt like I was moving the needle to make the workplace better because the resistance was too high. You recognize that the return on energy was so low. It was no longer serving me. It gave me headaches."

While some might have looked upon the upcoming birth of a child as a time to protect the stability that a full-time job provides, Kathy felt even more emboldened by how she was treated while she was pregnant. She was outta there.

Her bosses may have been babies, but they weren't on board.

"When I tried to quit and tell them that I was going to go build something for myself, they were like 'No, you can't quit.' And I said, 'Uh...I'm having a baby in two months...I'm leaving for maternity leave either way. It's just that I've decided I'm not coming back.'"

It was like she was speaking a foreign language to them.

"Their response was, 'Well, we need you to fly to Japan next week.' I was like, 'Did you not hear me? I'm having a baby!'"

Their response, however strange—and medically inadvisable—did make her wonder.

"What was funny to me was, at first, I didn't know if I should be flattered or horrified. Flattered because they didn't want me to quit and horrified because...well, that's obvious."

Flattery can be so insanely powerful. It's what makes us feel like we are the only person who can do this job, we are the special snowflake who was chosen and now I have this responsibility. If I left, everything would collapse and I'd be leaving my colleagues in the lurch and, and, and... all of these things you realize just aren't true when you leave a job. It's classic worst-case scenario thinking that leads to an inflated sense of self, however well-intentioned. I challenge anyone to say that they left a job and were irreplaceable, everything went south afterward, and their colleagues were never the same. I don't mean that we shouldn't have pride or self-worth; it's just that once we realize we really aren't all *that* important, making big decisions like quitting a job can suddenly seem like less of a big deal. We can stop inventing excuses.

Kathy had a hard time not buying into her bosses' apparent flattery. But she knew that, ultimately, it wasn't about her being good at her job; they weren't supporting her and her baby. She says it was a defining moment for her.

"It was two dads who were acting like what was in my stomach was a football or something not real. I had been thinking about leaving for a while. The timing wasn't great because I was about to have a baby, and there was a mortgage crisis.

And what does Kathy do after having a baby in the middle of a recession? She starts a business!" Her glee at taking such a big swing at life is infectious.

She had a lot of support around her, including her husband, whose advice was simple: "Just quit. We'll figure it out." Her friends, particularly her women friends and those who had started businesses themselves, were also fans of the idea.

"These were the people who had really had my back all along; it made me realize that I was never going to have that kind of support at work."

Kathy agrees that her ability to quit her job was an act of privilege in many ways. She knew she and her family would be okay financially if she took this risk.

Quitting is an act of privilege in many circumstances, especially when choosing to quit a job or career. Not everyone is in a financial position to accept the tradeoffs. I was able to quit that first job after graduate school because I had family support and the confidence that my education would make me employable again. I've personally felt that even quitting relationships can require privilege and stability in other areas of your life. The moment I decided to divorce my husband, I remember this flood of gratitude washing over me; I knew that I was able to make that decision for myself because I had an independent source of income, which meant I'd still have a roof over my head, food on the table, and the ability to get health insurance without a husband. Even the fact that my husband was not at all the type to make me fear for my life if

I divorced him is, depressingly, a privilege. But the fact that quitting is sometimes a privilege underscores the power of the shame and stigma it carries: even the most privileged among us (the wealthy, the white, the male), those who can accept all the tradeoffs and not suffer the same consequences, don't quit nearly as often as their advantage could afford them.

Kathy, like many happy quitters, has just one regret: that she didn't quit her tech career sooner. She knew ten years into her career that she was over it. But it took her another five years—and a pivotal moment with her frothy-mouthed boss—to work up the courage to leave.

"I'm not sure why I thought it was this scary, big decision," she reflects. "I guess you have this income, you buy a house, and you start to live at a certain income standard. If I could do it all over again, I would leave earlier."

Part of not quitting earlier also meant Kathy didn't feel like she had left on her own terms.

"They offered me a chance to come back and offered me more money, and I still chose to leave. It was never about the money! My boss actually sent me a bouquet of flowers after the baby came, and the card said, "Can you come back next week?" I really feel like you should leave when you know; don't wait five more years to do it."

Golden handcuffs are a real constraint for people and can make choosing to leave a job—and the lifestyle that comes with it—a debilitating choice. But the tradeoffs were well worth it for Kathy. And she forgives herself for waiting to do it.

"You do it when it's meant to happen and rather than beat myself up about it, I realize that those were the right conditions, the right set of circumstances, the right push that I needed to go."

She also embodies something that I felt deeply whenever I've quit something: it is forward momentum. It is progress.

"To me, quitting isn't a sign of defeat. I think it's a sign of recognizing your own power and energy and saying, 'This isn't serving me.' So, for me, it was really less about quitting as much as it was running toward what I wanted."

Even twelve years later, Kathy is proud of her decision to give up on her Silicon Valley career. She now has a thriving career as a keynote speaker and consultant, focusing on helping companies tell better stories and be more creative marketers.

"What makes me proud is that I handled it with dignity. I wasn't shown a lot of dignity by my boss, but I handled it with as much dignity as I could. And it was probably because that's the only choice that women and people of color working in tech had. I showed that I value principles and people over position. If I did it today, I think that I would still be dignified, but I'd also say, "Fuck you!"

We both agree that the "Fuck you" should be said in a very dignified, posh British accent and with a pinky in the air. And without spitting.

* * *

What if you hadn't quit?

"Oh, I had no intention of staying. So, when and what happened to me, it just made my decision easier."

What is the story you tell yourself about this quitting experience?

"That I had already known that I needed to leave."

What tradeoffs did you accept by quitting?

"Immediate income yet also knowing that I was leaving an environment where I could not flourish. So, all was good for me."

What does this quitting story say about you?

"That it was not quitting. It was choosing *me*. It's not so much what you walk away from. It's what you decide you are *for*. What are you running *toward*? And that was a choice to choose *me* and what was possible."

What makes you most proud about your quitting story?

"That I had the courage to take the plunge."

"I wasn't willing to put up with _____."

"I wasn't willing to put up with not being able to create the environment I wanted and needed to be happy and thrive."

I Quit the Circus

"Darling girl, when all else fails...join the circus."

UNKNOWN

Christina quite literally did "run away and join the circus." But it wasn't failure that led her there; it was actually a pileup of successes.

"I'm not nearly as optimistic about quitting as you'd think," she says, breaking my heart in the process. "I think of quitting as giving up. I think of what I did with the circus less as quitting and more about moving on to the next chapter."

Until our conversation, Christina had never actually said the words "I quit" in reference to her time in the circus.

Retired. Left. Moved on. Completed. These are all euphemisms for quitting that Christina uses more often.

"I moved on. I never quit." Now, she's just twisting the knife. "It was instilled in me, by society and culture, that giving up is

quitting. It has negative connotations. But it's all my perception, right? Like, realistically, what I was doing was quitting.
I quit school a semester before I graduated." There we go!

Christina had only gone to college to make her mother happy.
Once real-world job opportunities came beckoning, she felt
they outweighed the benefits of the education she was getting.

The real-world opportunity was a call from David Yurman,
the now-famous jewelry designer. She had been working for
him during college as part of a leadership program. The team
was asking her to stay on full-time and help open up their
first Boston boutique.

"I had always said to David's company that I'd go back to
school," Christina explains, "and they said they'd work with
me. But they put me on a leadership track, which is exactly
what I wanted. I never felt like I really needed a degree to do
what I wanted to do in life, and it worked out exactly that way."

She didn't need a master's degree—or even a bachelor's
degree—to get on the leadership track at what would become
the largest jewelry manufacturer in the world only seven
years later. As you might guess, Christina is quite capable of
forging her own unexpected paths in life. What I love most,
though, is how matter-of-fact and unapologetic she is about it.

"It wasn't the greatest choice in terms of making my mom
happy," she chuckles. "But it was one of the best life
choices I've made because two years later, I joined the circus. If I hadn't left college, my life wouldn't have gone in
that direction."

The story of Christina joining the circus is a lesson in seizing opportunities that present themselves in the moment.

As expected, she describes that life-changing moment straight-forwardly: "I walked into a furniture store, and instead of buying a couch for my first condo, I took a flying trapeze class."

A chapter of New York Trapeze School was set up inside Jordan's Furniture in Reading, MA. The school's motto is "Forget fear. Worry about the addiction."

This is so incredibly reminiscent of improv comedy's aphorism to "Follow the fear" that I immediately feel a nerdy kinship with Christina, even though my addiction to improv requires very little physical prowess and lots of beer after shows... hers required death-defying feats and keeping in great shape. One of my most favorite reactions I ever got when I explained to someone what I do on stage when I do improv was from my aunt at my bridal shower: "Why would anyone ever do that?" She was dumbfounded. I had no answer for her because, yeah, why would anyone get up on stage and be tasked with creating a whole show out of nothing *and* with making it funny?

When it comes to physical risks like trapeze, I have the same reaction as my aunt. But it was the motto that convinced Christina.

"It was the clearest moment of my life. I knew I had to do it."

The addiction was instantaneous for Christina, much like it had been for me the second time I tried improv.

She went from taking a couple of classes a week to taking them every single day.

"I was leaving the office for my one-hour lunch, driving twenty minutes north so I could fly for like ten minutes, only to get back in my car and drive back another twenty minutes to get back to work."

She didn't care that paying for classes made her go broke; she rented out her condo so she could cover the mortgage.

As Johnathan Lee Iverson, the youngest and first African American ringmaster in Ringling Bros history, has written: Compulsion is never convenient. Compulsions are a possessive thing.[3]

Christina went to China with her mother around this time to check out the trapeze talent. On the plane home, she informed her mom that she was going to work for Cirque du Soleil someday.

"She just laughed and said, 'Okay sure.' I said, 'No, I'm serious, I'm going to work for Cirque du Soleil. I'm pursuing flying trapeze, and I'm going to run away and join the circus.' She just laughed again."

Christina had been a gymnast and a cheerleader growing up but starting a trapeze career at age twenty-five would still be

---

3   Johnathan Lee Iverson, "Christina Cantlin Is Grounded...For Now," *Huff-Post,* March 16, 2016.

a tall order. It was now or never. She gave herself two years. She quit… I mean, "left" David Yurman.

"I remember turning in my resignation, going to my car, and crying," she says, "because I was free. I was happy. I didn't know what the future held, but I knew I was at least going to try."

She ended up moving into a house called "The Trap House" with other trapeze artists and working for the school.

Christina is certainly creative and does things her own way, but don't let that fool you into thinking she's not a driven, Type A planner. This former mathematics major got *analytical*.

"I was progressing in my skill, and I was very calculated from then on out," she remembers. "I started to research what other female trapeze artists in the world were doing, how you can go pro, and what sorts of moves sell. I learned that the double somersault sells, and only one or two other females were doing it at the time."

She also learned that the best female trapeze artists were part of multi-generational trapeze families.

"I knew that I had to get coached, not at this American school, but by one of these multi-generational families that know how to teach beyond a certain point."

Her circus career was unorthodox, as was her strategy to find a "family" coach.

"I basically stalked one of the most super-famous families in trapeze, the Gaonas," she laughs.

Her calls to them went unreturned. Then, she learned they were doing a summer camp in a suburb outside of Boston. She went there, a bottle of whisky in hand, and sat outside Mr. Gaonas's trailer until he came out.

Christina was, again, delightfully direct.

"I said 'I want you to coach me, I know I'm not your daughter, I'm not part of your family. What is it going to take? Money? I'm telling you I'm driven, I'm passionate, I'm talented, and I need you.'"

He told her it was going to cost her. She said she didn't care; she'd raise the money.

Christina certainly doesn't come across as a quitter, right? And yet, by this point in her life, she'd already quit college, quit placating her mother, and quit a career in high-end retail jewelry. It just goes to show that quitting isn't the death knell of ambition and purpose we often make it out to be.

She paid him for a two-hour private lesson.

"I went from an average flyer to above and beyond in just those two hours."

This got her hooked on getting the best instruction she could. She started finding resources all over the country to train with, including with one in New York, where she perfected the coveted double somersault and recorded it. Ringling Bros saw her YouTube video and came calling, asking her to audition. They hired her immediately, and she moved into the circus train. No college degree required. She was in her element.

"I started dating the catcher, I caught a double somersault in the show. It was amazing," she beams.

Cue the duh-duh-duuuuh music. Or a record scratch.

"And then I realized I didn't like working for The Man."

In Ringling Bros, each performer isn't hired by the show directly but rather by the person— almost always a man —who runs each act.

"I decided, I'd rather be *that* guy. I also learned that because I was the one of the few English-speaking performers, I was working more hours than anyone because I was also called up to do the media and PR tasks, like TV spots at 4 a.m."

The catcher/boyfriend had a relationship with a show in Japan. They decided to hire their own performers and leave Ringling. Christina became "The Man" who owned her act.

It was all part of her ultimate goal of getting to Cirque du Soleil, just like she'd told her mom on the plane back from China.

"I needed to be able to leave the train whenever I wanted and train whenever I wanted if I was ever going to make it there." She knew exactly what she needed to do, and she was going to do it.

Christina built her act in Japan and trained the performers. The 2011 earthquake and tsunami prompted a return to the United States, where she ran her own training facility in Alabama. Then, back to Japan, where she continued elevating her skills.

"I started to throw bigger tricks, like throwing the triple somersault and catching the double pike. That's when I felt ready to send my video to Cirque." It was four years after she'd taken her first flying trapeze class at the furniture store.

Two weeks after sending them her video, Cirque offered her a spot in their training program. It was basically an elongated audition, where she'd get to perform regularly in a non-Cirque show and get all of her room, board, and training paid. It was an incredible offer; at that time in the world, across twenty-six shows, there were only two female flying trapeze artists. Positions were hard to come by. Cirque wanted to train her to be available if a position opened up.

She left Japan and started training with Cirque du Soleil, including with one of their world-class trainers who had received the equivalent of a gold medal at the world's biggest circus competition.

Christina got hired for the Cirque show, *La Nouba*. She was there for ten months and met all of her goals, including throwing and catching the triple. She did each multiple times. Christina had done it.

"It was the best experience of my life. Once that was done, I was like, 'Okay, I checked that box. I can move on.'"

Some people quit things because what they were doing wasn't serving them well or at all; or because they aren't finding the success they'd hoped for; or they are fed up with not living their values and can't take it anymore. Christina provides a fascinating alternative: quitting precisely *because* you've been successful.

I admire someone who gets going once the going gets easy. There are plenty of reasons to be suspicious of billionaires these days, but one of my first mistrustful thoughts about the uber rich was always "Why the hell don't they just retire and let someone else make *their* billion?" It seems pathological to want to continue working that hard (assuming they are working hard, of course) when they have the freedom to do absolutely anything else. You did it, you're a billionaire, awesome… now, isn't there anything else you want out of life?

For Christina, injuries certainly also played a role in her decision. She had torn labrums in both shoulders and hips during her career. She was so passionate about it that, for many years, she didn't care what it did to her body.

"Four, five years later, I started to think 'you only get one body, so I guess I better take care of this one.' I started to understand my mom's perspective more. I had matured to a point where I understood, *of course*, my mother doesn't want me to fly a hundred feet in the air with only two wires. I get now that it wasn't that she disapproved or wasn't proud of me; she was mortified and couldn't bear the thought of me dying."

Christina had to re-evaluate her motivations.

"I had done everything I wanted to do, I had achieved everything I'd set out to. Did I want to keep doing this for the sake of doing it?"

Ever one to seize an opportunity when it presented itself, Christina took a chance when her stars aligned. Someone from her jewelry days offered an opportunity to go back to that world.

Quitting things can often come across as a selfish act; but Christina—and many others who quit things because they are not benefitting from them any longer—shows a common thread in many acts of quitting: generosity. Christina felt great about quitting the circus because she knew the community she was leaving behind would be taken care of by the new up-and-comers; she knew she wouldn't be leaving anyone in a lurch.

"The next step was just presented to me on a silver platter," she says. "When that happens, you have to take it. I did, and then literally everything happened for me exactly as I wished."

She may have done superhuman things as a circus performer, but Christina is still very much human. Choosing to leave the circus was hard.

"There was a bit of denial that my circus career was coming to an end. I went through all the natural steps: denial, anger, bargaining, acceptance. The real tough moment was when I realized that I had subconsciously set a goal for myself to catch the quadruple, which only one other woman in history has done. The only way I could have done that was if I stayed at Cirque and was surrounded by all that talent. I realized that I was never going to be in an environment again where I could become a better flying trapeze artist. That's when I processed that it was the end. But I accepted that everything, especially this amazing timing, was happening for the right reason." She had another crying in her car moment, this time crying to her mother.

What I immediately love about Christina is how matter-of-fact and unapologetic she is with her confidence and her security in who she is. She's someone who recognizes and appreciates her good fortune, but also knows she deserves it and is open with being grateful for it. She has the self-knowledge and self-worth to feel confident when it's time to quit.

She decided to "retire" and build her life back up. She put her analytical mind to work and decided where to build her post-circus life. She chose Tampa, Florida, because she ran demographics on the highest male to female ratio, most educated, and lowest cost of living to annual household income. "When I ran my search, Tampa lit up like a lightbulb," she says.

Sure enough, her planning paid off. She met her husband in Tampa.

"I am super blessed. My life just keeps getting better and better every day. I have an incredible career where I get to manage people and learn something new every single day. I work with intelligent people. I have an amazing group of girlfriends. I'm married to a beautiful, beautiful Punjabi man.

It was my birthday yesterday, and he bought me a car! I was like, that's a thing? People give *cars* as gifts?"

Christina is now what she calls "a normal person." No longer traveling the world, no longer living the life of a circus performer. She says her new life sounds boring compared to her previous one, but that she is incredibly happy.

"I quit my life to join the circus. And then I quit the circus to come back to my life."

She said she "quit." Twice. I'm so proud.

* * *

When do you share this story with others?

"All the time, it's my brand. It's six years later, and I still celebrate my retirement every March. I watch videos of myself and remind myself of what I was able to accomplish."

Any Regrets?

"I don't regret a single thing. I learned young that you regret the things that you didn't do. If I hadn't done it, regardless of everyone telling me at the time that I shouldn't, I would have regretted that."

What if you hadn't quit?

"The circus was great, but it was a bit of a bubble. If I hadn't left, I wouldn't have had the opportunity to learn all the things I've been able to learn not being in the circus. I would have regretted that. I have such a broader view of what you can accomplish in life now because I've been exposed to more things. Back then, I had a one-track mind. Now, I do things every day that scare me that aren't trapeze, like public speaking, investing money, and home improvements."

What tradeoffs did you accept by quitting?

"Being in the circus never felt like work. My job now sometimes feels like work. I occasionally think about the days when exercising was my job, and I couldn't believe I got paid for it. But there are other rewards now. Even on the days I don't like my job, it's because I'm being challenged or learning something new and getting smarter."

What makes you most proud of quitting?

"The fact that I did it [joining the circus] to begin with."

"I wasn't willing to put up with _____."

"I wasn't willing to put up with getting old. I wasn't going to quit my life or the circus just because I got older."

I Quit My
High-Powered Career
to Save My Health

Genevieve is the opposite of a commitment-phobe. She loves making and holding herself to commitments and gets peeved when others don't. She gets irritated when someone RSVPs to a party and then doesn't show, or when they RSVP "maybe." She follows through when someone suggests meeting up for coffee in the future and she agrees.

"I take seriously the commitments that I make," she says, with pride. "When I say yes to something, I say *yes* to it."

She feels that type of commitment and follow through has been lost, and she sees it every day in her work as a college career counselor. But she also sees it seeping into the behavior of peers her own age.

"There's a whole FOMO (fear of missing out) culture that leads to people worrying that if they say yes to something, they might be missing out on something else."

Genevieve recalls a time when even the busiest, most over-committed among us still made good on their promises. When she and her husband first met, many of their friends were "rocking it," in the political scene. Every Friday and Saturday night, their friends had five or more parties to attend. But they went to all of them, even just to say hello, because they said they would.

"It's something my husband and I try to do when we make commitments; if we say we are going, we are going. Barring an emergency, we show up."

But sometimes, even someone as committed as Genevieve reaches her limit and has to deviate from the path, she pledged for herself (and that others expect her to take).

"When other people were going like this," she makes an upward movement with her hand, like a plane taking off, "I was stepping away from things."

The "things" she is referencing is the bundle of commitments that came with her previous job as a consultant at one of the so-called "Big 4" consulting firms; a firm that claims itself to be harder to get into than Harvard, and the same one where I used to work. Genevieve and I were fellows in the same innovation program my final year at the company. I know what that bundle included: play hard and work hard until you have no time left to play and it's only work; sacrifice everything else you value in your life in pursuit of making your clients—and, therefore, the company's partners—happy. Achieve in order to achieve. It's not dissimilar to the saying about becoming a partner at a corporate law firm: "It's like you won a pie-eating contest, and the reward is more pie." To get promoted and eventually become a partner at our consulting company meant eating a whole lot of pie, your pre-diabetes due to lack of self-care be damned.

I had seen what lay ahead for me, and I didn't want it. Genevieve hung on a little longer than I did. While my disappointments looking at the life of managers, senior managers, and partners above us were more along the lines of "I'm not passionate enough about this to work so hard to reach the next rung in the ladder," Genevieve's decision to leave was intimately tied to something far more essential than passion: her health.

She'd been diagnosed with epilepsy right around the time she was "up" for promotion, as was the parlance at the company, from analyst to consultant; that would put her two rungs below Manager. The year you are "up" for promotion is definitely one that includes extra servings of pie. She was burning the candle at both ends, working extra-long hours in the evenings and on weekends while also contributing to the firm's extracurriculars. She was twenty-six at the time and working this hard felt normal to her.

But then she had a seizure. Many things can trigger a seizure, but as Genevieve was going through her diagnosis and meeting with doctors and getting lots of tests done, she learned that a trigger for some people can be prolonged stress.

A doctor asked her if she had been experiencing that recently; the answer was easy.

But Genevieve was young and passionate and had the energy for her demanding job, with a blue-collar Midwestern work ethic to boot; she was committed to climbing that ladder. And she managed to do it, excelling and reaching the senior consultant level all while fearing seizures and experiencing the occasional disorienting aura that required a coworker to escort her home. She was still at a junior enough level where she could have a quiet evening or weekend to decompress. She could read a book, maybe watch a movie, or even do nothing at all. She was able to adjust her life outside of work just enough to prevent more seizures. There was pie to be eaten, but it wasn't incessant.

Along the way, she also had a Manager or two who would support her and take the heat from partners for ensuring that she worked only forty hours a week to keep her stress levels at bay. But in the project-to-project life of a consultant, having a manager who could or would do that is never a guarantee.

"I remember talking to someone in HR about my diagnosis and my needs, and she asked me, 'Okay, so when do you think you're going to get back to normal?' When I tried to inform her what a chronic illness and disability is, she just said that maybe this company isn't the right place for me." There was not going to be a world at this firm in which she would not be expected to work seventy hours a week.

But she persisted for the next several years, eager to get promoted to manager. Every once in a while, her husband and her family would ask her to give it a think.

"They can recognize when I'm not in a healthy place," she says. "They would remind me that I want to be around for my daughters and my husband in the future, and I'd question if the job was really worth it."

My heart sinks when she says her husband got in the habit of asking her if she had cried at work that day.

Eventually, Genevieve knew she had to make a last-ditch effort to see if there was any possible way she could stay at the company. She scheduled a meeting with her partner, with whom she was close, to tell him she was thinking of leaving the same year she was "up" for manager. She says it was one of the most difficult professional conversations she's ever had.

"He was really surprised and first said something about how the company had just gotten done investing in me with this fellowship for a year, and now I was going to leave?"

But Genevieve was a high performer, so the conversation quickly led to what it would take to make her stay. He asked what she needed. A new project? A new client? Money?

Genevieve knew exactly what she needed. She knew she couldn't do what she needed to do to become a manager and still be healthy.

"I need a forty-hour workweek," she said.

"I can't promise you that," he replied. "If it were anything else, I could do it."

Genevieve knew this was the case; she'd been at the company six years and had never seen anyone above her get offered less pie. She knew she'd been there long enough to have given it her best shot.

"Deciding to quit when you are at the top of your game is really hard. I know I had what it takes to become a partner, but at what cost to me?"

After quitting, Genevieve made a series of what she calls "lateral" career moves. This wasn't in her nature and took some getting used to.

"I've always striven to be the best, to be the top, to continuously grow, and to achieve. Living in a city like Washington, DC, you are always looking for that next step up. Now, I'm a Type A person trying to fit into a Type B personality. This has meant quitting and saying no to a lot of things in my life."

While she acknowledges her decision to quit her consulting career and become a college career counselor meant going downward in terms of salary, she also has clarity on what the upside has been: "Things have gone upward in terms of my quality of life."

She loves the predictability of her schedule and the school year; that the built-in breaks are for everyone; and being in an environment that values the pursuit of knowledge for the sake of understanding rather than profit. Her boss actually gets upset if anyone on her team emails after 6 p.m. or over the weekends.

"I find when I get home," Genevieve says, "I am a better mom, wife, and friend. And, for what it's worth, I cannot remember the last time I cried at work."

Genevieve often uses her own experience with trading off prestige for quality of life when she counsels her students on their own career paths.

"I work with a lot of very high-powered, Type A students who want to be Secretary of State by the time they are forty." She knows that many of them are mainly attracted to the glamour, the power, and the prestige of their dream careers. "I can look at my past with the perspective of a career coach and know when I should have maybe listened to a different little voice in my head or made a different decision."

But she knows that experience is often the best knowledge to have and maintains empathy for her students' ambitions.

"I feel like I always have tried to make the best decisions I can at any one point in time with information that I have."

* * *

What if you hadn't quit?

"If I hadn't quit the company, I think in some ways I would have been fine. I enjoyed the work and was good at it. I was really starting to step into my own niche and become known. But, at the same time, I didn't want to risk the very real threat to my health. I also saw myself becoming a person I didn't recognize. Instead of bringing out the best in me, the competitive aspect of the firm was bringing out the worst in me, and that is what I found most frightening of all."

What is the story you tell yourself about this quitting experience?

"I made the best decision I could with the information that I had. For me, the tradeoff in less pay was worth the promises of health. While I wasn't able to escape my epilepsy (in fact, at my next job I had two seizures in two years), I didn't know that at the time. I was looking out for my health and my family and made my decision based on what I thought was healthy for everyone."

What tradeoffs did you accept by quitting?

"Less pay, less prestige, and accepting more lateral career moves."

What does this quitting story say about you?

"It says that I recognize there is more to life than power, riches, and prestige. Health, true-time with family, and time for rejuvenation are being lost in our consumerist world. The ability to step away from the rat race shows (and I know this sounds a bit prideful) wisdom."

What makes you most proud of your quitting story?

"I did what was right for me and my family, not what the world said was the best thing to do."

What values does this quitting story say you have?

"Wisdom, self-knowledge, balance, mindfulness, love of family."

"I wasn't willing to put up with _____."

"I wasn't willing to put up with my health going into decline to line a partner's pockets."

I Quit Being a Doctor

Yvonne had a very multicultural upbringing. She was born in London and was raised in Nigeria and the United States. When she returned to the US for high school, her family made it clear what was expected of her: nothing less than the "American Dream."

"It was very much implied that 'you're going to go to America and you're going to do all things,'" she says. "And you have only five boxes. You can either be a doctor, a lawyer, an accountant, an architect, or an engineer. That's it. Anything outside of that is…well, you don't even talk about that option."

I absolutely know this story of preordained choice of what is "acceptable." My parents were (and are) way less traditional than most South Asian parents I know, but even with their lenience, I grew up aware of only three available career boxes: doctor, lawyer, and engineer. Ah, the luxury of having *five* choices!

Yvonne grew up with a lot of Indian friends and a steady diet of Bollywood movies, so she also sees the parallels between the expectations of her Nigerian culture and mine.

"We share this idea that you can only be one of these things or else you're not enough or not smart."

Smarts weren't Yvonne's problem. She was first in all of her classes and was, especially being the oldest child, the golden expectations-setter for her cousins.

"There was always this expectation that I was going to go somewhere and do big things. 'Big things' meant bringing honor to the family by excelling in one of those five acceptable professionals." For Yvonne, "doctor" was the obvious choice.

"I was smart, but also very empathetic," she remembers. "So, when you have that combination of being good in school but also caring toward people, it was easy to expect that I would become a doctor."

She was also already developing a humanitarian streak.

"Growing up in the developing world, I would see kids dying from preventable illnesses. A cousin of mine died from pneumonia. A child I used to babysit when I was home from school died from lack of access to care. I was very, very interested in public health because of this. I had that inclination to help people, and medicine seemed like the only way to do it. Medicine was always the plan for me."

She was as gifted in music as she was in science and math. But no one ever dared suggest she pursue music.

For little girls, though, being smart often comes at a price.

"I wasn't very domestic growing up," Yvonne says. "I was always reading a book. So, my identity very early on was formed by hearing people tell me that no one would marry me, but I can be whatever I want because I'm smart. But all I'm good for is books." She laughs hard at this.

I share Yvonne's lack of care about this notion that a woman can either be smart or appealing, but never both. I remember when I wrote a love note to a boy whom I had a crush on in sixth grade. I wrote it while sitting on the (closed) toilet in the guest bathroom. I imagine it was a good place to have privacy and not be bothered while I wrote to Matt that I "liked him" on small, white stationery with three red hearts across the top. A few nights later, one of Matt's friends called me at home and told me Matt didn't like me because I was "a nerd." I remember just saying, "Okay" and hanging up. Goodbye, Matt! See you soon, sweet, sweet spinsterhood!

Yvonne's intellect wasn't just recognized by her school or her family. Her country saw it, too. She was one of only two children from her state that were sent to Nigeria's first gifted school.

Being around the smartest of the smartest kids only solidified her identity as an intelligent, high-achieving young woman.

Yvonne praises her experience at the school, calling it very enriching, enlightening, and even powerful. But she also now calls the worldview it created "completely skewed."

"It was only about how smart you are and how much you can accomplish."

The gifted school offered music and other artistic classes, but Yvonne focused more on math and sciences because of the perception that they were more difficult.

"It was more of a status thing to be good at science and math," she says. And, of course, she was good at those subjects. She was bringing honor to her family by doing all the "right" things excellently.

Through what Yvonne will only describe as a "series of crazy and traumatic events" she ended up going to the US at age seventeen to join her mom, who had moved to North Carolina a few years earlier.

This was when the expectations for her to achieve great things got a name: The American Dream. For her, the dream absolutely had to become a reality.

"My mom had been a banker before, and in the US, she had to start all over, cleaning toilets. So, there was that additional pressure on me because I was young enough to do it differently."

Did she ever.

She excelled in her American high school and won all the awards. But she didn't forget about her love for music. In fact, it played a big role in her applying to medical school.

The day she decided to apply, she was on a high from finishing her music demo earlier in the week. She was speaking with her mother-in-law, who was reminding her that it was time to apply now that her year-long "break" to work at a medical lab was over.

Yvonne went to her computer soon after to find out application information. She found that but also something else: a sign.

"I opened up the Association of American Colleges and Universities website, and right there on the front page was an article about doctor-musicians. It was about all these doctors who play in bands after seeing their patients. I was like, "Oh wow, there's a way for me to do both, be a doctor and a musician! That article made me apply to medical school."

The same week she learned she got into medical school, she also got a record deal.

"But, of course, it wasn't enough to just be a med student!" she laughs, remembering the audacity of her own ambition. She declined the record deal.

Yvonne also got a prestigious fellowship that allowed her to have her own HIV outreach project. She trained other med students to go into the community to do rapid HIV testing for people in soup kitchens, homeless shelters, migrant clinics, and more. It was such a successful project that it became a full-fledged organization. She was running a community health organization while she was in medical school!

Her idols were Oprah and Albert Schweitzer, the namesake of the fellowship she was awarded. She went on lobbying trips to Washington, DC, to advocate for things like universal health care and children's health, all while excelling in her medical school classes.

"We were like rock stars," she says of herself and the other Schweitzer fellows. "I, especially, was this radical wild card. I went to medical school to help people and change the world. I was an unapologetic idealist."

She knew she was doing incredible things.

"I was just this kid on fire. I wanted to be a dynamo who did humanitarian medical missions. And I was crushing it." Throughout medical school, she didn't forget about her passion and talent for music; she performed in all the school talent shows.

Yvonne says her time in medical school was a lot of fun. I come from a family of physicians, and never in my life have I heard anyone call medical school "fun." You'd think Yvonne had found the exact right place in the world for herself. She did too.

Then, just as she was finishing up her fourth and final year of medical school, she learned she was pregnant. But that didn't change her ambitious plans one bit.

"I was still in that mode of, 'Okay, I'm just going to do what I've always done, which is keep going one hundred miles an hour.'"

Yvonne had her daughter a couple of months before graduation. That's when things changed.

"I really started to think about why I was doing what I was doing. Was I was doing it because I really wanted to? Or because it was always expected of me?"

Yvonne's doubts about her motivations to be a "dynamo" will be familiar to almost every happy quitter or to every person who is dissatisfied with their life. So many factors—society, family, the pleasure of being good at something—conspire to prevent us from understanding and going after what we truly want for our lives. The deck of pressures is stacked against us, which makes quitters that much more admirable.

She started to really look at medicine and reflect on why she went into it. It was transformational.

"I've never been the same since," she says, solemnly.

What she realized was that yes, she was motivated to help people, and she was able to do that to her heart's content while in medical school. But her residency in internal medicine and pediatrics proved to be different. She had chosen those two specialties so she could eventually go travel the world and treat both adults and children. Her experiences as a resident soured her ambition.

"I was spending all my time in the hospital but not even seeing patients," she says, frustrated even now. "I was spending more time on paperwork and being embroiled in the hospital politics. I felt like just a cog in a machine. I wasn't making a difference pushing paper and seeing patients for only five to seven minutes. It was just like, 'What the hell am I doing? This is not why I went into medicine. This is chaotic and this is harming patients.'"

The grueling demands of residency and its thirty-six-hour shifts at the time also impacted her family life.

"I was gone from my kid all the time. I saw her for only one or two hours a day. If I wanted to see her more than that, I'd basically have to stop sleeping the two or three hours I was able to get each night. I was taking care of other people's kids in the pediatric ward more than I was taking care of my own."

Yvonne's life was completely out of alignment with the ideals that had originally brought her to medicine: to be the "dynamo" that was helping others.

"As an idealist," she says, "it's important for you to live the values that brought you into your work. And here I was, around people I admired, and they are all tired and burned out. Nobody likes what they are doing, and all the language around you is discouraging."

I understand this dissonance well. My father was a radiologist, so he didn't even see many patients. I grew up hearing him complain and say bad things about his job. Every time he was called by his technicians to review an x-ray, it elicited a stream of foul words from his mustachioed mouth, words that quickly became a part of my linguistic repertoire. He was probably irritated by all the same things Yvonne eventually hated too, plus the perverse incentives for medical professionals that don't always prioritize patients. But "doctor" was one of the three pre-approved professions in my culture. Like Yvonne, I was "smart." Compared to my older brother, I was the good student, the one who had a chance at getting into medical school. So, when my dad came to me when I was early in high school and suggested that I go into medicine, I was like "Are you kidding me?" The pressure of that too-short list of acceptable professions was strong enough that it could make you recommend someone you love to dedicate their lives to something you hate. Fun fact: my brother became a doctor later in life! He seems to enjoy it far more than our dad ever did.

Just like my dad, Yvonne was, at a young age, preordained by family and circumstance to become a doctor. Unlike my dad, she would not stay one.

"It was around the time they changed the residency shifts from thirty-six hours to twelve hours," she says, recalling the momentous shift in how medical residents were treated. "I was working in the intensive care unit. People were leaving their shifts without signing off to the next group of doctors that were coming in, so patients were just crashing left and right. This was my first time in the ICU and I was like, 'What is going on?' One attending physician scolds you for doing something, but what you did was exactly what the previous shift's attending had told you to do. It was just chaos." She shakes her head in disappointment.

One night in the ICU, Yvonne was caring for a patient that was crashing, and she couldn't find her "senior" anywhere. The attending physician was yelling at her for doing what the previous attending had told her to do before they had left. She'd gotten only two hours of sleep a night for weeks.

Something in her snapped.

"I was just like, 'I can't do this.' It was a very clear moment. I was done."

It was the first time in her life Yvonne had quit anything.

The sunk costs of becoming a doctor can feel very real. Many people sign up for hundreds of thousands of dollars of debt, knowing it may be five to ten years before they start making a good living.

Yvonne doesn't mention the sunk costs of time and money as factors that made her quickly turn her "I quit" moment into a half-quit, but I have to imagine it could have played a role.

"I said to myself, 'okay, maybe this feeling I have is temporary. Let me take a break and come back to it later.'"

True to her high-achieving norm, taking a "break" for Yvonne meant getting a Master of Public Health degree at Johns Hopkins.

"Getting an MPH was a way to show the world that I wasn't quitting medicine, that, 'It's just this moment over here, I'm going to go do this, and don't worry I'll come back, and I'll be good!'"

But two things happened during her master's program that turned her half-quit into a full quit:

First, she loved what she was studying. It included courses in personal and professional development and in managing non-governmental organizations. In one of her courses, she read *Daring Greatly* by Brené Brown. Yvonne was hooked.

"In that book, she talks about how the space between your professed values and your practiced values is burnout. For me, that was the statement that described where I was as a doctor."

Yvonne became really interested in the idea of burnout and started to focus her studies on that. She began to pursue positive psychology and coaching certifications. She spent the three and half years of her MPH program soaking up all she could about her new passion.

During her program, she learned she was pregnant with her second daughter. Though she had no doubts about completing her MPH, she wasn't so sure she could finish her residency with another infant at home.

Then, just as she was about to complete her master's program and return to her physician work, her father passed away in Nigeria.

They had been estranged for much of her life, had reconnected ten years earlier, and had kept in touch by phone ever since. Yvonne learned that he had gone into a coma. While he was in a coma, the doctors in Nigeria went on strike because they hadn't been paid in months and felt they were being mistreated. They started discharging all the patients, including her dad.

"I was here, in the US, trying to coordinate his care in Nigeria and trying to figure out where they sent him. 'Where is my dad?' He ended up in a rural clinic somewhere and was dead within twenty-four hours."

For Yvonne, her father's death was caused by an uncanny combination of what she was dedicating her life to at the time: physician burnout.

"This is what it looks like when burnout is taken to the Nth level," she says about the Nigerian physicians' strike.

She became haunted by the idea that what happened to her father could happen in the United States. She decided to make her capstone project about physician strikes.

That same year, she visited her in-laws in San Diego. The morning after she arrived, the front-page story in the local newspaper was about a physician strike happening in the University of California Health System.

"That is when I knew for sure I wasn't going to go back to my residency," she says. "I knew that if what happens in the developing world starts to happen here, it's going to be catastrophic."

The same year her father died, a family friend who was as accomplished and successful as Yvonne jumped off a bridge during her own medical residency.

"For me, this was becoming a recurring theme of what happens when you don't quit and when you stay in a toxic situation. People either kill themselves, or they kill others."

She learned that physician suicides are quite high; nearly four hundred per year are known. That number is the equivalent of an entire medical school.

"I needed to stop and pay attention."

She did stop, and the result was the clarity needed to commit to the quit. Her life as a doctor was over.

Yvonne describes this feeling like a "muzzle" finally removed. That year was rough, but opportunity also knocked in that same time period. Someone contacted her about wanting to quit medicine. They had seen Yvonne's story on Facebook.

"She didn't even feel empowered enough to tell me her name. She told me her story using a pseudonym."

Even the most accomplished among us feel muzzled by the shame that swirls around quitting. Sometimes, we place the muzzle there ourselves. Other times, people in our lives try to do it for us.

"We ended up moving to San Diego and I was planning to start my coaching and speaking practice there. When we got there, it became very clear that my husband and my in-laws were against what I was wanting to do. They gave me a lot of pressure to go back to medicine or public health."

She didn't. Her husband divorced her.

It's noteworthy that her husband and his parents were not Nigerian... or South Asian. They were white Americans.

Their expectation that she stay in the medical field was likely tinged by race dynamics.

"It's like, 'Okay, so you married a Black woman,'" Yvonne surmises. "It felt like part of the appeal is that I'm a doctor and that makes me 'enough' for a white family."

Everyone around Yvonne was so invested in the idea of her being a hyper-accomplished "dynamo" that they couldn't see who she really was or what she valued. Her own family's reaction was devoid of understanding.

"They couldn't believe that someone as hardworking and 'gritty' as me couldn't save my marriage. It was as if I was too weak, too 'American' to fight for my marriage. I had to deal with everyone else's baggage around quitting."

Her family remained in denial about her no longer being a doctor for a long time.

"I was the oldest in my generation and quite the trendsetter when it came to achievement. When I quit medicine, it was cataclysmic for my family. I still get calls from family members telling me about openings at hospitals."

Yvonne now coaches full-time, specifically coaching mission-driven physicians and other professionals through burnout.

"I help people who want to quit to get off that edge. And I help them quit in a way that works for them, so they feel supported in their decision."

She estimates that 90-95 percent of the people she works with are physicians. She holds free weekly respite sessions for medical professionals who are working on the frontlines of the COVID-19 pandemic response.

She's made a career out of advising people on how to quit because she has regrets over how she did it herself.

"I quit without a safety net. I just jumped. And I ended up divorced and homeless with my kids."

Her experience colors her current view of quitting immensely. Although she grew up with a "never quit" environment in Nigeria, one that took great pride in African "grit" and felt quitting was an "American" thing to do, she hasn't gone fully over to the other side of things when it comes to quitting. She's not a "burn all the bridges to save yourself" person because of what happened to her after she quit medicine.

She's also come to realize that quitting is a privilege for many people.

"If you're an immigrant, a woman of color, or have a lot of student loans or other debts, it's nearly impossible to take a break from the profession, let alone quit. So, people will end up being exploited or they might take their lives. I've learned that there is privilege to burnout; there is privilege around being able to quit."

Before writing this book, I hadn't pondered how quitting can sometimes be an act of privilege. To take a leap of faith and quit a job or an entire career requires a certain amount of financial and societal privilege. Getting a divorce or leaving a romantic partnership does too. It only makes me wonder why so many people who carry so much privilege (I'm looking at you, straight, white, cis, men) don't exercise that privilege and quit things right and left. The social stigma and shame around quitting is just that strong.

Yvonne is an advocate for quitting the "right" way: a way that leaves you with options and with your dignity intact. She urges her clients away from the desire to "blow things up" like she did; to consider what support they have, if they have enough money to tide them over, how they plan to survive after the quitting is done.

"You can't quit just to end the pain. You have to know what you want in its place."

I don't think there is one "right" way to quit. There are as many "right" ways to quit as there are quitters; it's an incredibly individual decision to know what "pain" is worth it. But I do think working to understand your values so you can determine if what you are quitting violates them is the surest way to avoid regret.

Yvonne learned that being good at something wasn't enough to continue doing something that didn't match her values.

"I can't imagine practicing medicine even though I was great at it," she says. "I'm done pretending to be somebody I'm not. I used to have to dim the lights within me to fit and be taken seriously. Now, I have such a passion and a fire about life. I'm in a place where I'm using all of the things I'm good at. I even start my speeches by playing guitar and singing."

* * *

Any regrets?

"I wish I could have found a way to ask for support about how to come back. But nobody cared if I stayed or if I went. There were no advocates. I don't regret leaving medicine at all, but I do regret not being able to leave in a way that supported me."

What if you hadn't quit?

"I would have probably killed myself."

What tradeoffs did you accept by quitting?

"I had to be okay with the constant disappointment from my family. I had to make peace with that. I had to make peace with the years where I was just financially strapped."

"I gave up a lot of prestige, status, respect and power, influence, and authority. After I left, it was like my words meant nothing to people."

What does this quitting story say about you?

"It says I have the power of my intuition and how connected I am to it, and that I am able to recognize my path."

"It says that I am one courageous, intuitive person."

What makes you most proud of your quitting story?

"I'm most proud of the difference I'm making now. Nearly every single day now, I get direct feedback on the impact I'm making in other people's lives. I am leaving a legacy. I know that I am affecting generations. That is super humbling, and I'm really proud of it. I'm really proud of the freedom to create."

What values does this quitting story say you have?

"Purpose, integrity, authenticity, curiosity, adventure, service, altruism, and, really, wanting to be of service and wanting to live an aligned life authentically and showing up with all my values."

"I wasn't willing to put up with _____."

"I wasn't willing to put up with an inauthentic life. I wasn't willing to put up with mediocrity. I wasn't willing to put up with being a cog in the wheel and not making a difference. I wasn't willing to put up with profit over people. I wasn't willing to put up with not being there for my kids and not being fully present for my life."

QUITTING IDENTITIES

I Quit Being a Mormon

———

Amanda self-identifies as a "perfectionist," a trend I see in many people who are now happy with their ability to make decisions about quitting things in their lives. Much like them, Amanda lived a life of doing the "right" thing… until she didn't, and it opened up a new world of possibilities for her. But quitting was something she had to learn.

"I would actually say, in general, I don't quit," she says emphatically. "I put a lot of value on finishing what I start. My favorite thing to do is to finish something. That's why, if I listen to a podcast, I'll never start in the middle; I have to start from the very first episode, even if it's not a serialized podcast. If I'm reading a book series or watching a TV show, I'll want to finish the entire series even if I'm only kind of liking it. I'm a very goal-oriented person."

Amanda and I agree that the worst thing about e-readers is that you can't easily learn how much progress you've made toward finishing the book; the tactile, visual feedback an actual bookmark gives you is so much more satisfying. It's like a waving flag telling you how many more laps you have until the finish line you will most certainly cross.

I recognize Amanda as a fellow "completionist." We both get joy from finishing things, following through on our commitments, and the reward of closure. I'm so grateful to see these qualities in Amanda, who is a nurse. I hope "good at follow-through" is a trait all medical professionals are expected to have.

There is no doubt that Amanda's sense of duty and doing the "right" things were considerably informed by her Mormon upbringing. She is the sixth of eight kids with a temperamental father who had Obsessive Compulsive Disorder. The Mormon Church offered many privileges that could be taken away if they misbehaved, such as not taking their version of Communion or not being permitted to get married in the temple if you had sex before marriage. The worst risk was being excommunicated entirely. Being seen as a sinner and losing respect were ever-present dangers.

"I realized in the last couple years that Mormonism is a religion based on perfectionism," she says. "In fact, one of the tenets is that you are supposed to try to be like Christ, who is perfect. So, every day you're trying to get more and more perfect. It's also a very goal-oriented religion, which is a good thing and a bad thing."

I can't help but think of Mormonism as a cosmic video game where one is constantly trying to "level up." I wonder if this type of competitiveness—or, as Amanda says, the "goal orientated" nature—is unique to proselytizing religions.

Amanda had plenty of role models among her rebellious older siblings for how *not* to attain perfection.

"I didn't know this at the time, but my oldest sister, who is eleven years older than me, was in juvenile detention and even in jail. She was a sex worker; I only learned this later, but when she got pregnant and gave the child up for adoption, the father was her pimp. She left the church, was doing drugs, and was in and out of rehab a lot. And my other sister got pregnant in high school. Another sister was well-behaved in front of my parents but was sneaking out all the time and partying."

Yet another sister was defiant to both her parents and the church, often doing drugs and regularly running away from home.

It's easy to imagine what this type of "imperfect" behavior created at home.

"My dad is definitely a volatile person and cares about obeying the rules. So, there was a lot of yelling, a lot of punishments, and spanking of my older siblings. I saw my older siblings being 'not good' and getting punished by my parents, and so I thought, 'Well, if I just do this, I won't get in trouble, or if I don't do this, I won't have those issues.'"

Amanda now believes her perfectionism was a coping mechanism for the anxiety that came with never thinking she was good enough in her family or in her religion.

She did all the right things when she was young: got good grades, participated in the church, and brought respect to herself and her family. She was permitted to get married in the temple in her early twenties as a virgin. Even though she didn't want to have children, she knew that she would have them because that's what was expected. She did everything correctly, everything people told her she should do, including marrying a fellow Mormon.

Her marriage was also connected to her educational ambitions. She met and started dating her husband while they were both students at Brigham Young University, where she majored in theater. At the time they were casually talking about marriage, Amanda missed some deadlines to renew her full scholarship. Faced with sitting out a semester or two of college and applying again, she instead decided to apply for scholarships in her boyfriend's home state, Oklahoma. She got a full ride! And this made the decision to get married pretty obvious. Mormons usually don't move across state lines with their boyfriends. They had their temple wedding in Oregon that summer and moved to Oklahoma the very next day to start both their classes and their new, married lives.

Amanda had followed all the rules and met all the expectations of her church. But there was one tenet that she soon realized was missing.

"No one said you should also choose the right person *for you*."

Within the first week of being in Oklahoma, it all came undone.

"He was acting really strange, and I started to joke with him, asking 'Hey, what's going on? You don't regret anything do you?'"

One day that week he replied: "I regret marrying you, and I don't think I love you."

They were living in an apartment her husband's father had made for them above one of the truck stops he owned; it was right next to a cattle farm and across from a pig factory. I can only imagine the smell. Amanda was stuck in rural Oklahoma, far from her family in Oregon, with few days of classes under her belt. She hadn't yet made any local friends.

"I was so devastated, and I didn't know what to do. In the Mormon Church, you think you're going to be married for all eternity; you die, and your spouse, children, and everything about your family continues on."

She didn't tell anyone about her marriage falling apart one week in. She didn't know how to talk about it with anybody; nothing about her upbringing had prepared her for how to react when things didn't go right or for when her hard work and obedience didn't pay off.

But, true to form, she continued trying. They went to therapy together. She still tried to be a "good" wife, which included continuing to have sex with him. She still went to church.

"It was the perfectionist in me. I wanted to say I had done everything I could. But once I'd checked off all the boxes on the list I made inside my head, it still didn't make a difference on his side."

She stayed and continued her classes for a few months.

"I didn't want him to screw up my education, too."

I know this feeling of being in a place that is not yours, the one thread connecting you to it, abruptly cut. I broke up with my neglectful, long-distance college boyfriend a week before college graduation, a week before I was going to move from New York City to Bloomington, Indiana, for the summer while he finished up his classes there. I spent three months living alone for the first time in a three-bedroom apartment, working several jobs, and trying to make friends with townies. I drove to my parents' house in Ohio every single weekend, knowing my eyes would be sufficiently dry from all the tears shed during the week. I think I watched every hour of the Beijing Summer Olympics. I often refer to that summer as the worst of my life. The only positive was discovering how hot male water polo players can be.

Amanda finally told her parents about her failed marriage in November. She went home to Oregon that Christmas, by herself, and never went back to Oklahoma.

Her husband called her right after she left, mea culpa-ing all over the place.

"He told me all the right things I was waiting to hear." He was saying he didn't know what he was doing and was crazy to end their marriage. "So, I said, 'Okay, I'll find us housing at BYU because we were going to transfer back over there.'"

He called again the next day. This time to say he regretted what he'd said the day before.

"That was the final breaking point," she says. "I'd given him every chance. I just had to go home and deal with this emotionally."

Divorce in Mormonism isn't actually as controversial as it can be in other religions like Catholicism. Amanda had gotten married in Oregon, so she had an alternative: annulment.

"Oregon allows for annulments in a few different scenarios, including if there was some kind of deception. He said he didn't love me and had never loved me. So, he essentially lied to me, which counted as deception. He didn't contest it, so we got the papers together quickly, and it was done by February or March."

Amanda's marriage was over. But the biggest change to her identity was right on her heels.

"This was the first time I started rethinking my faith," she says. "I felt like I had done everything right, and everything the religion promised me didn't come true. I saw my sisters, who had been sex workers and done drugs, happily married. I was like, 'Whoa, what happened?'"

As a person who was brought up to feel that her "goodness," her perfection, was within her control, Amanda felt betrayed.

"The end of my marriage wasn't my fault. I felt abandoned by God. I felt like, when I prayed after that, I wasn't getting this thing that I always thought I was going to get in return."

She still considered herself a Mormon, but she started getting other perspectives, primarily through dating non-Mormons and spending time with their families. She saw plenty of non-Mormons being…well, *happy.*

"I was dating a guy who was from a big Catholic family," she remembers, "and I was at a party at his parents' house, and there were all these kids around, and aunts and grandparents, cousins, and friends just drinking beer and having fun listening to the music. I remember thinking to myself: 'none of these people are unhappy.' I realized everything I thought was true was not true. I just never knew it because I was only ever around other Mormon people. The whole idea of my religion was that you can only be happy if you are Mormon. I learned that was false."

I'm reminded of what French philosopher-writer-feminist Simone de Beauvoir wrote in one of her memoirs about her observations of her own religion at a young age: "…it seemed to be that believers and nonbelievers led just the same kind of life."[4] Another hyphenate de Beauvoir soon added? "-atheist."

"I remember being at his house," Amanda says, "and wondering what would happen if I didn't go to church. One day I just didn't go…and then I skipped it the following week… and nothing happened. I was waiting for something bad to happen to me for not showing up, and nothing did."

She passed the cosmic test and never went back.

---

4   Simone de Beauvoir, *Memoirs of a Dutiful Daughter* (New York: Harper Perennial Classics Modern Classics, Reprint edition, August 2, 2005)

Was it impossible for both things to be true, for her to remain a Mormon *and* believe that non-Mormons can be good and happy?

"The Mormon Church has such a belief that everything in their doctrine is the only truth," she explains, "that if just one of those things isn't true, then it all falls apart. That's the problem with saying all of your stuff is true. Because if just one thing is false, then it throws it all out the window. If A doesn't make sense, then B, C, and so on also don't make sense. I'm an all-or-nothing person."

This house of cards Mormonism built was no match for Amanda's perfectionist, completionist streak. I imagine her deciding if she couldn't do it "right" or go all the way, then she wouldn't do it at all.

As she began to form her own identity without Mormonism, she started to call even more bullshit and solidify her decision to quit   `.

"I started to question the patriarchy a lot more than I already did, and I was already feminist for a Mormon. I started to realize that just because my father said something, I didn't have to do it. He wasn't in charge of me. I definitely lost respect for that whole idea of men having authority. I always knew I didn't want to be a mom, but when I was Mormon, it was just so expected that I was sure I would have kids. It was a relief to realize, "Oh, I don't actually *have* to be a mom.""

It wasn't just patriarchy in the home that she outright rejected.

"Patriarchy is a big tenet of the Mormon church; its whole premise is that the man, as head of the family, gets the revelation from God via male bishops, male wards, male prophets, and so on. The second you question male authority, you come to the conclusion that everything the prophet said he heard from God is not true."

During her departure from her faith, Amanda was able to read some texts that were banned by the Church, including some scholarly biographies of Church founders.

"We were always told that men marrying fourteen-year-old girls was just a function of the 'olden days,' that the man was just trying to give the girl a good home, or that this was just a story. You read these historical texts and you realize that, just as with all other cult religions, this is statutory rape!"

She was also disturbed to connect the dots between Mormonism and racism, citing how Black men were not permitted to be priests until the late 1970s.

"We were told, 'Oh, that's what God wanted.' No, that's racism!"

Her love for and involvement with theatre also presented a moral challenge. Amanda had known plenty of (most likely closeted) gay people during high school and college when she acted in plays and musicals.

"The big tenet in Mormonism regarding LGBTQ issues was 'hate the sin but love the sinner.' That never felt right to me, but I had to believe it."

Quitting the Mormon church represented Amanda's ability to be truer to herself.

"After I quit, it was like, 'Oh wow, all of these things that I feel at the core of me, I don't have to justify anymore. I can just say all these other things are bullshit.'"

For Amanda, doing the "right" thing ultimately became doing what was right for her and for her own values, even though it meant sacrifice.

Amanda is still a driven, goal-oriented person, but she's learned to let go of her old perfectionist attitude toward life.

"So much good in my life has come from quitting. It's something that I've had to learn. You have to accept that sometimes you will fail—whatever that even means—and sometimes quitting is actually the healthier thing to do."

* * *

Any regrets?

"I don't really believe in regrets because every stone you touched led you to where you are. The experience of leaving the church eventually brought me to Bob, my husband. It's hard to have regrets because it taught me that you can't be perfect even if you try. It taught me that it's okay for me to question and decide what *I* want. It's okay for me to have the kind of marriage I want where I don't change my last name because, 'fuck you, why should I?' Every part of life teaches you something or makes you who you are, so how can I regret it too much?"

What tradeoffs did you accept by quitting?

"I'm lucky that my family aren't the kind of Mormons who would disown me for leaving the church, but I'm definitely not as close to my parents because of it. And I'm less close to my siblings who have stayed."

"I also gave up the comfort of thinking there is some all-knowing being who loves you and will help change your life for the better and also protect you in the afterlife. I had to get over that, and it's hard at first to think, 'Oh wait, this is it. No one's there to help me.' That was a weird change in philosophy for me."

What does this quitting story say about you?

"Quitting Mormonism says that I set limits to further my own happiness and that I have good boundaries. It's given me real optimism; I can live in the now."

What makes you most proud of your quitting story?

"I think I'm prouder now that I can be very verbal and passionate about the rights of people that I would have had to be quieter about if I was still in the church."

"I wasn't willing to put up with _____."

"I wasn't willing to put up with untruth. I wasn't willing to hear anyone who was going to tell me that God is going to bless me more than my sister who was a sex worker, because that's not true. I wasn't willing to be told that my place was in the home and I needed to have children. I wasn't willing to be told by some guy that God told him the only family that is legitimate is one with a man and a woman who are having kids."

I Quit Evangelical Christianity

———

Chase describes himself as a "bad Millennial" for having stayed in the same job for a decade.

"I'm someone that will try to push through things no matter how difficult," he says. "'For me, it's fear of the unknown. It takes so much energy to start something new. I am really impressed when someone quits a job because it's not the right fit for them."

Like many people who have grown up in the United States, the culture of youth sports strongly framed Chase's view of quitting.

"If I were in a sport and I became nervous or anxious and I wanted to quit, it was like 'No you stick it out no matter what.' In my family and our culture, you never quit; you stick it out even if you are uncomfortable."

The idea of loyalty and commitment was also ingrained in Chase outside of sports.

"There was this idea of, 'You don't get to dictate the terms of how things are going to go in life,'" he remembers. "It's this sense of parental, 'If I had to stick it out, now you have to stick it out. You don't get to decide how this goes.'" This is how the shame and stigma around quitting becomes generational.

I write elsewhere in this book about the "fatalism" in my own family, this sort of throwing up of hands and "What can you do?" attitude. What Chase mentions adds a veneer of indignant revenge; because our parents (or whoever) had to live through life being told not to quit, suck it up, and *this* is what loyalty and commitment look like... because they suffered, we have to suffer, too. I'm sure every generation deals with the exact same thing, but perhaps it's more noticeable in our current culture because Millennials—those of which Chase says he's a bad representative—are often maligned by older types for their lack of loyalty to jobs, relationships, and cities.

What I see in Chase's and my experience, though, is this sense that our parents didn't get the luxury of choice... therefore, we also shouldn't. How dare we try to avoid the suffering that is our inheritance? My dad had to decide to become a doctor when he was in eighth grade. Despite him moving to America, in part, so his kids could have more choice, whenever we avail ourselves of our freedom to make those choices or pursue change, it makes him anxious. This is especially true when it involves quitting relationships or jobs. He still wishes everyone could just find that "one, stable" job and stick with it. Or just move to Columbus,

Ohio, and "settle down." Is it mere discomfort with change? Natural, understandable parental fear? Envy? Probably all of the above. Quitting might be the life choice that carries the most stigma, perhaps because it has the most uncertainty attached to it.

But then again, my dad left his childhood home and lived in four different countries across three different continents, and, oh yeah, fled a country in the middle of the night to escape a murderous dictator...all before he had me. His current "change is something to be worried about" stance was probably rooted in his inability to experience—even sometimes seek—stability as a young adult. It's interesting he doesn't have a greater sense of ease for his own children's very comfortable "big" choices, all of which have taken place in one country (but not Columbus, sorry Dad). I suppose change and choice aren't always the same thing; my dad, perhaps, didn't experience a lot of choices, but he did experience great change. Meanwhile, I have great choices, but my changes are laughable compared to his. Honestly, he should be making fun of me for how soft I am and how faux-important my little life upheavals are. Change isn't always a choice. But quitting – and not quitting – is.

In every attempted takedown of the Millennial generation and how they have no loyalty to [fill in the blank] or ability to just suck it up and take it, all I've ever noticed is jealousy and rage: *how dare these young people figure out what's important in life decades before we did?*

Chase lived this. "Hard work was a value in my family for sure, but what was underpinning that value is a kind of cynicism: 'I had to go through this shit, so you have to, too,'" he concludes.

Fear also played a huge role in Chase's biggest quitting decision: leaving evangelical Christianity. In fact, it was fear that drove him to become "born again" in the first place.

He was raised north of Dallas, Texas in a religious, Protestant family. They went to church regularly, and it was a big part of their culture. Around age nine, Chase decided to be born again, which is a really important step in evangelical Christianity. It means you have renewed your commitment to God.

Chase's motivation to be born again was, initially, more about running away from something he feared.

"I was afraid of going to hell," he explains. "And that was how the message from my church was delivered. That if you aren't born again, you'll be separated from God and everyone you love. And Hell is this dark hole, a place of terror, of torture."

The fear of a literal hell, instilled in him by Christianity decades earlier, is palpable for Chase even now.

"To this day, I can't watch movies about demon possession without feeling really shaken. As a kid, to be possessed by a demon felt like a real threat to me."

I feel so sad and concerned imagining little Chase in his bunk bed worrying that he could be possessed by evil at any moment and face eternal separation from his God and his family.

I'm an atheist, but even I have to think, "Oh my god, yes! Of course, go get that born-again demon protection, little Chase!"

He was only "loosely" connected to his church for a couple of years after he became born again. When he got to middle school, the bond became much stronger. He got more involved in his church's youth group and started studying the Bible and proselytizing. He and his fellow church members would speak in tongues and participate in faith healings where the "laying of hands" was perceived to cure all sorts of ailments and maladies.

The church youth group also had a lot of social value for Chase. It was a place to have friends and hang out. He played guitar for the youth group band. They had a drama team. Church offered a lot more than just religion.

I remember being in middle school myself, a South Asian in rural Ohio, and suddenly realizing the worst fear everyone has at any age: my friends were all hanging out without me. It started when, for about two weeks every summer, all of my friends were gone. I later deduced they all attended church camp. But even during the school year, there were a lot of things that I just didn't have access to because they were happening in my friends' youth groups. By far, my biggest crush in middle school and high school was an Archie Andrews lookalike. Imagine my disappointment when I learned that "Archie" wanted to be a youth group pastor when he got older. There was never going to be room for lil' ole' budding-atheist me in his world.

I understand what youth group meant to Chase as a community precisely because I was always on the outside looking into that tight knit space.

But Chase had another motivation, besides a social community, to get more engaged with his church and its youth group: destiny.

"It's clearer to me now looking back, but there is this egocentric aspect to thinking that God has a destiny for you," he reflects. "It was preached a lot that God has a great plan for you to do great things, and that really motivated me to be involved."

I'm going to come clean: I became an atheist because, after a few years of seeking and searching a variety of religions in middle school, I didn't like what I found. In general, what I found was condescension, groupthink, blind obedience to authority, sexism, and more. I'm not a fan of any of those things. I've never been one to care about what happens in the afterlife or how we got here to begin with; I'm more concerned with what I do with my time here and now. I have greater respect for non-proselytizing religions like Hinduism (there is no conversion process) and Judaism (they make it super hard to convert) than those that try to conquer the world through conversion. I'm certainly no religious scholar, but I feel like when you let just anyone in, the quality has got to erode, right? Because I live in America, I see this erosion most when it comes to Christianity. I see how poisoned American Christianity has become in my lifetime by people who don't really live the principles but still get to call themselves "Christian." Maybe Christianity would be better if it were more like an exclusive nightclub with a dress code instead of a Target on Black Friday. How about some QC for the JC?

The first time I said, "Aw, hell no!" to Christianity during my middle school years was when I participated in what I think was called a "Russian bible study" with my friend, Cara. Apparently, at some point in Russia's history, to be a Christian was illegal and so they had to meet in secret and at grave personal risk to worship and pray. Cara's youth group scheduled a weekend church "lock-in," which was basically a big, co-ed sleepover for all the kids in the church's giant gymnasium. But to get into the gymnasium, we had to "break-in" to the church just like those persecuted Russian Christians. I remember literally belly crawling through the dirt by the side of the road while "guards" (church chaperones) pretended to try to catch us with flashlights. It was all very dramatic, but it was also kind of fun!

My experience with the idea of proselytization is very much bound up in my ethnicity and the way I look. I have brown skin. Jet black hair. Dark eyes. What could politely be called a "generously 3D" nose (please be polite). I am most definitely not white. To the young Christian kids in that gymnasium, and in countless other situations in my youth, I was a flashing neon sign that said, "I'm not Christian! Come convert me!"

Cara and I "broke in" to the gym, and the fun sleepover stuff began. Music, soda, snacks, board games…Midwest church gymnasium luxury! Within minutes, we were approached by three or four girls who quickly turned the conversation to "We'd love to share some Bible passages together." "Sure, why not?" "When in Rome" might be an inappropriately pagan, Jesus-murdering phrase to invoke here, but that was the spirit I had at the time. I remember going upstairs to a quieter spot on the second floor with the group of girls and sitting on the carpeted floor in a circle, cross-legged. Some Bible passages were read out loud. Then one of the girls suddenly asked, "Coonoor, can we pray for you?"

Here's how one hundred percent atheist me would respond to that question now: "Bitch, I don't need to be prayed *for*! You can pray *with* me, but what is it about me, besides the color of my skin and your assumptions about what religion I am, that makes you think you get to condescend me like that? Bitch, if you let yourself be curious about anything besides your own world, you might learn that there are more Christians in India than there are people in this shitty state that you will probably never leave! *Bitch.*"

I was more polite (passive? cowardly? ignorant? unself-aware?) back then, so I just said "yes" and we all joined hands. I'm sure I didn't close my eyes while they prayed for my heathen soul because group eye-closing has always been weird to me.

Every time a Christian has tried to "save" me, they've stressed what a "personal" relationship they have with God and how amazing it is. I always wonder, "If it's so personal, then why are you sharing it with me? Can't you just be confident in what you have with God and let me eat this damn sandwich?" I feel like there is a unique insecurity in adherents of proselytizing religions.

So, I bristle when Chase mentions the "great things" God had in store for him. I assume this means he was part of a community that encouraged head-in-the-sand obedience and rejection of other ways of thinking. I'm wrong.

"Believe it or not, my experience with the church taught me to be a really critical thinker," he says. "This church I was in was like, 'You need to examine the Bible on your own and come up with your own opinions.'"

Chase took this to an extreme level compared to his peers. He didn't just examine the Bible; he went down the rabbit hole and read numerous books *about* the Bible. He became a bit of a Bible nerd.

I also cringe because I assume Chase's religious fervor meant going off to convert and "save" people who his church decided need saving.

On this, I'm not far off.

"I was really entrenched in the church and the youth group because of this idea of compassion. Like, you don't want anyone to go to hell, right? So, you want to bring them into your fold. We'd especially focus on the outcast kids," he explains. Chase sincerely felt in his heart that he was doing the right thing at the time.

I definitely lead my life using my "head" rather than my "heart." I prefer to think rather than feel. Verbalize rather than stew. Externalize rather than internalize. I remember needing to tell my first therapist to stop asking me where in my body I was feeling that thing I just talked about. I'm a robot (sociopath?) made in 1981 who, just a few days ago, needed to cry but couldn't until she/it had had three glasses of white wine. Emotions are hard. White wine is an excellent diuretic for emotional constipation.

So, it's amazing to me to hear Chase describe how the *feeling* he got in his church was also an additional motivation to be committed to it. He'd experience these feelings especially during "praise and worship," where everyone in his church would gather together and sing directly to God and Jesus.

"It's one of those things that is difficult for anyone to study or measure, but during those gatherings, I did have instances of very, very euphoric feelings," he says, smiling at the memory. "I felt this wholeness and this peace come over me. You can't argue with that feeling. It kept me involved for a really long time."

Chase describes different circles of Christian fervor like this:

- An outer circle for whom Christianity is more of a club and a cultural identity; it's just something that they do. Chase is dispirited when he says that most American Christians today fall in this circle because of Protestantism's dovetailing with nationalism, white supremacy, and capitalism.
- A middle circle for those who are seriously committed to the teaching but also want to have a life that might include having kids and earning a lot of money.
- An inner circle for whom the teachings are really internalized; there is a mystery, and they are trying to figure it out. It's in this circle where you find the adherents who are likely to sell all their possessions and go proselytize.

Chase fell squarely into this inner circle; he truly felt his future was about living as Jesus had. He was on track to be an itinerant preacher.

He certainly wasn't alone in this inner circle, but in high school, he realized just how different he was from most of his peers.

His youth group was invited to a leadership conference in Washington, DC. He shared a room with his good friend, Manny. Chase and Manny were pretty popular in the youth group. They both fed off each other and reinforced each other's faith and leadership qualities.

One of the conference sessions they attended was a session on ethics. It was led by (you couldn't make this up if you tried) Tom DeLay, who is notable for two things: being Republican House Majority Leader from 2003-2005 and being indicted and convicted on criminal charges of conspiracy to violate election law by laundering campaign money. You know, Christian stuff.

There was also a conference session that included a really intense discussion about spiritual warfare; how there is a linear timeline for getting to the end times and the reckoning, and "what are we Christians all going to do about it?"

"I took it to heart," Chase says. "I couldn't imagine just being a street preacher. I asked Manny, 'what do we do about this?'" Manny was offended: 'What do you mean?"

Manny wasn't trying to be an all-in Christian. He wanted to have a career and have a regular life, eventually. He wanted to have fun.

"That really underlined how entrenched I was. Here was this person who I thought was on the same page as me, I thought we were in this spiritual fight together. Up until this point, I thought everyone around me was matching my sincerity."

Chase's spiritual devotion to God had physical implications as well. A Texan through and through, he also played on his high school football team. He remembers once doing a three-day fast and only drinking juice to get a closer connection to God. He and his church friends went to the mall to proselytize, something he chuckles about now. But he was supposed to be putting on weight for football.

This football versus church tension created a rift between Chase and his father.

"Without me even realizing it until much later, my youth pastor was becoming like a father figure to me," Chase says. "I think my dad was more aware of it than I was, and he was kind of jealous of the connection we had because he and I were never very close."

At that time, Chase's dad was in that outer circle of Christian fervor.

"My dad couldn't understand why I'd fast during football season when I was supposed to be putting on pounds. He told me he didn't want me to fast, but I still did it and lost twenty pounds. It was a real point of contention between us."

In high school, Chase was in an evangelical play called "The Worm." He played the main character who, throughout the play, is forced to relive all the opportunities he had in his life to accept Christ and didn't. In the play, his avatar is in hell watching him relive all these missed opportunities.

Even though I perceived Archie Andrew's religion as a barrier to me making him my boyfriend, Chase's romantic partnerships were decidedly more diverse than you might expect. And it was one reason why the wheels started to fall off for him when it came to his religion.

"I was always pretty open when it came to romantic relationships. I wasn't ever very cloistered in that way or only dating other believers."

One of his most serious high school relationships was with a Persian woman whose family was mostly agnostic.

"They were amazing, beautiful people, and I really admired their approach to life," Chase remembers. "It was a struggle because I wanted her to be saved. But she was a good person, really caring for other people, and she really enjoyed life." "What, exactly, did she need to be saved from?" he wondered.

Chase continued to encounter more and more people like her in his late teens, those who were leading a "Christ-like" life, even though they weren't following Christianity or fearing eternal damnation.

He was starting to contend with the inherent contradictions in his faith. He was meeting more people who were good in the Christian sense, but who were not Christian. His religion compelled him to save them, but they didn't need saving. Something had to give.

"I was also seeing more examples of Christians who were living lives that I didn't respect because they were living it as a cultural identity rather than a deeply held belief."

Chase and I observed the same corruption to American Christianity happening at the same time, at the same age, but in two very different states.

Chase's extended family also gave him reasons to doubt what his religion had to say about nonbelievers.

"I was curious about the world and wanted to travel and learn about other people and cultures," he says. "My extended family wasn't into exploration, learning, or curiosity in a way to which I felt drawn. I think I began to see reflections of what Christianity was in that area and time in them, and it wasn't as appealing to me as what I had seen in my agnostic Persian girlfriend."

Chase brings up this inherent contradiction that exists, in different forms, in every religion: how do you reconcile going through the world "knowing" that everyone who doesn't share your belief system, which is a majority of the world, is ultimately going to "hell"?

But millions of Christians—some of them close friends of mine—acknowledge this contradiction and remain secure in their faith. Why couldn't Chase reconcile the discrepancies? Why did he ultimately decide to quit the evangelical Christian church after being so devoted nearly his entire life? So devoted that he was, at one point, ready to live the life of a penniless preacher?

"Well, I remain a Bible nerd to this day," he says. "I still read a lot about it. I recently read about this biblical scholar who was so into the evangelical church that he learned Hebrew and Greek so he could read the original scriptures. And through that process of learning, he became a nonbeliever. This resonated with me a lot because I felt like I had a similar experience. You start out by being told that this is the word of God and there are no flaws in it. I was encouraged to examine and investigate. I feel like the more you research and the more you educate yourself, you see the fabric start to fray. Once you see that it can't possibly be the all-encompassing truth, then you start down a path of potentially leaving it behind."

Chase, much like the scholar he mentions, could be said to have experienced the "wisdom paradox" in which greater knowledge leads not to greater certainty, but rather to doubt because of how much you realize you don't yet know.

His youth group had a maxim of "You will be the same person you are today five years from now, except for the people you meet, the places you go, and the books you read." Chase took that as instruction and pursued people, places, and books earnestly; all of which resulted in him leaving the church.

But Chase is honest about how his other, less than pious, Manny-esque aspirations also motivated him to quit the church.

"My motivations weren't totally altruistic," he admits. "I wanted to be able to go to college and not just get an education but also have life experiences. I wanted to drink and have sex. I wanted to be someone who was open to 'sinful' experiences, and it was hard to reconcile that with how the church tells you to live your life."

Chase was growing more and more certain he could have these "sins" in his life and still be a compassionate person. But he still grappled with his decision well into college. He remembers yet another romantic experience during his junior year of college that gave him clarity. By this point, he had what he calls a "progressive Christian attitude." He was politically liberal, not going to church but trying to hang onto his spirituality.

"I remember my girlfriend was cutting my hair on the porch. I found myself telling her that I had essentially left the church and was no longer practicing the religion. I remember this emotional, dramatic feeling when I said it out loud," he tells me.

My parents may disagree, but I didn't grow up in a religious household. My mother is certainly a practicing Hindu and prays every day in her home mandir and does fasts when required; my dad changed his "faith" regularly when I was living at home, sometimes declaring he was Hindu, sometimes Muslim, sometimes Buddhist. Let's just say I was trained at an early age to view self-proclamations of belief systems with skepticism. I have become a "show, don't tell" kind of person because of this.

All this added up to my surprise at the reaction I got when, during a visit home soon after college, I casually mentioned out loud that I'm an atheist. I didn't even think it would be controversial in my family. But it was my dad who was taken aback and shocked. Sad, even. He said, "It doesn't matter what you believe, but you have to believe in God." I understand since then the gravity and importance of saying out loud "I'm an atheist" and not shrouding it in anything else. If Bible thumpers can walk right up to my door and try to convert me (which they do) why can't I tell the world that I'm an atheist? I like to show *and* tell my atheism now.

More recently, Chase was at a party, and the conversation turned to religion. Even though he identified as a nonbeliever, he still struggled to say, "Jesus is not the son of God." The language of his former religion remains so ingrained.

He is still drawn to the idea of a spiritual fabric existing and uniting everything. But what draws him are things like meditation and Buddhist teachings, things that can be applied to a secular world. "The compassion aspect still appeals to me, just within a different paradigm," he says. He likes things that drive him to sympathy and self-reflection.

"Another thing that's really moved me along has been how awful the evangelical church has been for political life in America," he says. "It just highlights all of the issues I was having with the church in the first place. If you support Trump, you're not a Christian. From a doctrinal perspective, it's just black and white." I'm inclined to believe a self-professed "Bible nerd" on this one.

"Right now, I could go somewhere and toss a rock and hit someone who I don't think is actually living a Christian life but says they are," he remarks.

He says he still prays, but that it's more like he's praying to himself. When someone close to him is, say, going to the hospital, he tries to send his mental energy their way.

"There's a belief in me that, on some level, we are connected in some way."

I'm still a proud atheist. But even I do what Chase describes. I don't think of it as praying, but I do find myself thinking/saying/wishing things like:

- There's no way that people who are about to die in an airplane crash just sit there and feel all the physical pain of having pieces of a giant tube of metal tear into their flesh, right? Or drown in a capsized car? Some force just gives them some mystical cyanide, and these poor people get to "go" before they have to suffer? I hope for a cosmic euthanasia that prevents pain in these circumstances.
- When I'm lying in bed at night with the love of my life, my three-year-old Bernese Mountain Dog, Nikka, next to me, I'll whisper to her: "Please stay with me a long time." I'm saying it to no one, I know. And I know it's futile. But I say my wish out loud, anyway, because I want it so badly it hurts.

I don't pray, but I have intense hopes.

Chase traveling and meeting people from different backgrounds in his twenties continued to cement his distance from Christianity.

"I was meeting these great people who were maybe Muslim or gay, and I really respected these people, and I looked up to them.

After bringing good people into your life and bonding with them in a sincere way, why would you then say, 'Oh, by the way, you have to come to my side when it comes to religion.' I didn't want to change any of these great people who entered my life."

Chase says he's gone the route of agnosticism instead of choosing a different religion.

"I think the way I pulled apart from Christianity wouldn't have allowed for that kind of devotion to another religion. The same issues would have been there."

Chase only recently told his parents that he is agnostic, after years of dropping hints.

"I backed it up with all these reasons, like if you take an intellectual look at the Bible and how it was put together, and all the historical flaws and issues that exist within it, how some books were clearly not written by the author it's attributed to...," he trails off.

He was armed with every reason he had, every experience that had informed his decision over two decades. But his parents still think he's on the path to an eventual homecoming to his faith.

"My mom will send me information on new churches in my area that look 'cool' and encourage me to check them out... they'll say they are praying for me."

They are praying "for" him. Chase is now as much on the outside as I was in that church gymnasium.

His wife continues to demonstrate what he started to learn in high school: people can be good without religion. She isn't religious, but her job is focused on helping others, she volunteers, and she's good to her family.

Chase has a constant reminder every day that compassion can exist without compulsion.

* * *

When do you share this story with others?

"I like discussing religion with people in general but especially what connects people to religion. It's so intertwined with the political discussion right now. I'm very vocal with how disappointed I am in the evangelical church being conservative in the first place. Supporting someone like Trump is baffling. It brings to the surface this question of 'what *is* the evangelical church?' If these people are supporting Trump and his policies, then they clearly don't understand the religion of which they are a part. If you're looking at the New Testament, the bulk of the teaching is compassion and charity. For them to miss that and instead focus on abortion and gay marriage... they don't know what the hell they believe in."

Any regrets?

"It's really hard to say. My process of quitting was a gradual one, and I was a different person at each point in that progression."

What if you hadn't quit?

"My family sure would be happy. But I'd be living in a world that would be a lie to a certain extent. Because I had such a struggle with it for so long, I can't go back and pretend it's all kosher."

What is the story you tell yourself about this quitting experience?

"It's still evolving. Early on, I was hard on myself and felt like, 'Oh, you just can't live the life that is required of you.' But, primarily, I benefitted from forming relationships with non-Christians, having deep bonds with them, and learning from new people."

What tradeoffs did you accept by quitting?

"The negative was losing community in a certain sense. And losing somewhat of a stabilizer. I'm someone who needs that inspirational, meditative thing on a regular basis because I had that growing up. I miss having the transcendent feeling that I would get in church and would help me rest for the week. I can feel that sometimes with meditation, that sense of peace comes over me, but it's not with a community. I also gave up having a code that I could fall back on if I was anxious or scared. I have my own code now, but back then, the code was just given to me."

What does this quitting story say about you?

"Honesty and authenticity matter to me. I have a devotion to truth. Let's live in a world where we don't have to make things up to make ourselves feel better. The principles I learned in the church are what brought me out of it."

What makes you most proud of your quitting story?

"Being open to becoming someone that is quite different than the environment I grew up in."

What values does this quitting story say you have?

"Truth. And having an authentic life."

"I wasn't willing to put up with _____."

"I wasn't willing to put up with contradictions."

I Quit Being a Softball Star at Fourteen

Quitting is usually a response to a negative outcome or experience. We quit people because they are failing us. We quit jobs when they start to make us miserable. We quit identities we realize we never chose. In general, we quit when something is failing us or when we are failing at something.

It's unique to quit when you are excelling at something you were born to do. That's exactly what Phoebe did when she decided to quit her sports career when she was fourteen years old.

I've started to wonder if the main reason our conceptions of quitting are formed in childhood is because so much of growing up (at least in Western culture) is about competition: sports, grades, activities, essay contests, scholarships, piano competitions, choral contests, student council elections, band competitions, play auditions, and more. These are things I recall from only my own childhood, and I was lucky enough to grow up in a pre-helicopter parent era and live in a place where there were no good private schools nearby, you'd have to sign over your first-born for them to attend.

So, childhood is rife with opportunities for us to learn things like "never quit" or "quitters never win," a veritable breeding ground for such toxic thinking. Phoebe inherited this "wisdom" a lot as a youth athlete. Her parents instilled in her a strong work ethic, and while they weren't extreme "win at all costs" types of parents, they did expect her to finish things she started.

"They were never like 'you need to be the best' or 'you need to get the best grades,'" Phoebe says. "But even if you are in last place, you have to finish."

When you become an adult, you are suddenly without all of the structures and systems in place that coordinated competition for you as a child. There are far fewer forums in which you are contending with others. Adulthood is much more about challenging yourself. And to do that, you have to find out what you want and what motivates you. Phoebe is unique because she did this at a young age.

Phoebe was born into a sports family, a softball one, specifically. They lived and breathed softball. Her dad was a coach, her mom was at all the practices and often served as "Team Mom," and her older sister played through high school. There were practices twice a week and games on Saturday. In addition, Phoebe and her dad would practice together, throwing balls in the front yard or going to the field to practice batting. At one point, her sister came home after college and helped her dad coach Phoebe and her team.

"It was a real family affair," Phoebe says, "It was our lives. It was just something you were expected to do." She started playing softball when she was six years old. By junior high, she was the head pitcher. She was on traveling teams and named to All-Star teams. Her teams always placed first or second.

"Softball was always who people thought I was, and it was how I defined myself."

At that age, it's so easy to become "branded." You're the jock or the popular girl or the class clown or the nerd or the exchange student or the kid who fell off the stage during *Our Town*. It's easy to be perceived as only one thing and have that become a self-fulling prophecy.

Phoebe was "the softball player" for years, but she started to question if this sport was for her the year she turned fourteen. A game when her sister was home floods her memory.

"My sister was first base coach, and my dad was coaching third. I had batted and gotten to first base. The next at-bat, my sister told me to run to second. But I was sizing up how the pitcher and the catcher were communicating with each other, and I said 'No, I'm not going to second.' Because I was a pitcher, I knew it wasn't a good situation and that I might get into what's called a 'pickle' and be stuck running back and forth between first and second. My sister is yelling at me 'Go! Go! Go, Phoebe!' and I became just so fed up in that moment." Phoebe rolls her eyes in exasperation as she tells this story, frustrated even twenty-some years later by how her opinion didn't seem to matter.

Pride was definitely at play as Phoebe began reconsidering the life she'd been born into.

"I felt like I'd been doing this for seven years, and I knew what I was doing. I've made a ton of different teams on my own. I've impressed coaches. And you're going to yell at me like a child? It was a suffocating moment."

An independent streak was also at work.

"I had plenty of knowledge by then, but I still wasn't making any decisions for myself."

It can sometimes be hard to remember our thoughts and opinions from when we were young, but Phoebe is extremely clear about what motivated her to quit being "the softball player." This wasn't only about rebellion against family dynamics and asserting her independence as a teenager.

"I didn't like who I became when I was competitive," she says. "I noticed that I got really mean, I got agitated. I would get forceful with people. I didn't like that about myself." There is regret in her voice as she says this; she still feels bad about this behavior.

She describes the expectation that players would yell and ridicule the opposing team during games. But many of the girls on the other teams were Phoebe's friends.

"When you're playing, it's like 'you're my enemy.' It felt like such wasted emotion. I didn't fit in in that way."

She remembers the teams from her part of the state being stereotyped as "tomboys," while teams from the coastal cities had a different reputation and suffered the consequences.

"The girls from the coastal towns would show up with their boyfriends and have lipstick and blush on, have their nails done. And we would just break them down so hard. It was weird."

There was another moment when Phoebe felt especially uncomfortable with her own mistake. "I was pitching, and I hit this one batter in the head. It's easy to assume that pitchers are capable of doing that on purpose, but it's actually demoralizing for a pitcher. Because if you hit someone, it means you didn't have the control or the craft to throw a specific pitch that would trick them into swinging. Real pitchers don't do that shit on purpose because it says more about the pitcher than it does about the person who got hit."

Everyone assumed Phoebe had hit the girl on purpose. The girl happened to be unliked by the others already and was hysterically crying. Phoebe recalls the other girls making fun of her and laughing.

"I was just so upset by that. I hadn't done it on purpose or for people to laugh at this person." Phoebe sounds scandalized. To think people would consider she'd done this on purpose made her feel awful.

I think back to my own years playing softball. I played for a few years after graduating from T-ball. I recall being somewhat decent at catching and second base. Hearing Phoebe's story makes me so grateful that I went to a school that wasn't known for its athletic prowess; nasty competitiveness isn't something I remember. The only injury I ever got while playing softball was when a few of us were bored waiting to bat at practice. My teammates started leapfrogging over their metal bats; two hands on the handle, leap over. I blame this on being shorter than the others, but on my first try, my vagina landed with a painful *thud* on top of the metal handle. There was blood. I had to wear a maxi-pad from my mom that night. It was cruel practice for when I'd get my first period a couple of years later. Tennis, with its lack of contact and petite hitting implements, became my sport of choice.

While fear of physical pain factored into my decision to drop softball, Phoebe's reason was more emotional.

"It just reached a point where I said, 'I might be good at this, but it has turned me into a person that I don't like.'"

Excelling at something wasn't enough for Phoebe to sacrifice her values and morals.

Phoebe quit when she got to freshman year of high school. That year, she was offered a spot on the junior varsity team, no tryout needed. She said no.

Phoebe had no nerves or doubts in telling her parents about her decision to quit the family business.

"I was just like, 'I'm doing this. Next?' I think by that point, I'd just had enough that I didn't care what they thought."

Phoebe was taken aback by their lack of reaction to her decision. They weren't upset so much as they were perplexed and a bit doubtful that it would stick.

"I was ready for a backlash, to get skeptical questions about what I was going to do instead, to be guilted by how much time and energy they'd put into me, or get reminded of college and softball scholarships. But none of that came up."

The family had a new focus: Phoebe's older sister just had a baby.

"They were all juggling other priorities. My sister was starting her family, and I don't think I was their main concern because I was always pretty obedient and was getting good grades."

What did come up, soon enough, were little comments and reminders here and there. Things like "So and so from your traveling team made varsity at Carlsbad High," and "So-and-so just got a full ride on a softball scholarship."

"They did care," Phoebe admits, "but they were very passive, aggressive about it. It was a marathon of reactions to try to get under my skin. I basically walked away from who I was, or at least who I thought I was. I didn't quite understand how much of an effect it would have on my family when I quit."

Phoebe embraced the independence from her family's sports identity right away.

"It signaled to me, 'Hey, you can do things on your own. You can actually sculpt out your life the way you want to.

You don't have to be who your parents think you should be. And by the way, those friends that you have? If they're not going to be your friends after softball, they're not your friends anyway.'"

She soon found dance and theatre and dove into performing, something she does to this day as a writer and actor.

She remembers when one of her softball friends got a scholarship to Mississippi State, and her mom spoke about it like it was incredibly prestigious.

"By that point I wanted to move to San Francisco and be a writer, so all I could say is, 'That's great!'" She mimics a comically forced smile.

Phoebe laughs thinking back to the disconnect that happened between what she was starting to value as a huge part of her identity—the arts—and what her family still cherished.

"They were like "What is this?" It was hard for them to get on board because they didn't understand it." But her quitting softball especially changed her relationship with her dad. Gone were regular team practices and the one-on-one sessions they'd have together.

"I traded off more one-on-one time and conversations with my dad, for sure. During high school, we had a real communication breakdown. If I had stuck with softball, maybe the breakdown wouldn't have been as intense as it was. It took my mom dying [years later] for him to want to talk to me like I'm a person. He might have seen me walking away from softball as an affront to him." As Phoebe processes this, I don't sense a hint of regret in her voice.

"I don't think my dad came to a performance of mine until my senior year of high school."

That performance was a competition, of course. And Phoebe won in her category. There were trophies. But not all competitions and not all trophies are created equal.

"The drama trophies end up in the drama room. But the sports trophies were displayed in the principal's office window," she says, resigned to the unfairness of it.

She still has her softball trophies.

"They are in a fucking plastic box. Who cares? I'm not going to put them up in my house!"

Another thing Phoebe isn't going to do? She won't sacrifice her personal integrity or values, even if it means defying expectations or risking relationships. She learned to stand up for her values and live them by quitting at such a young age, which is remarkable.

* * *

Any regrets?

"There are times that I think I could have gotten that college scholarship. It also seemed that, in my particular city, a lot of athletes had an easier time in honors classes. So maybe, if I had stuck with softball, I would have been treated better by the teachers, or my coach would have advocated for me. Maybe my academic life would have been a lot different."

"I don't regret that I did it. I would do it again because that decision empowered me to move forward in a direction and led me to the place where I'm at now. And I'm pretty happy right now. So, I know that if I hadn't done it, things would have been a little different. Maybe I wouldn't have found theatre. I came into the drama program as a freshman, and I established myself pretty quickly. By sophomore year, I was getting lead roles. I don't think I would have been able to gain those roles if I had made my decision to quit softball later than I did. And because I got out of the jock crowd, I met all these amazing people that I am still friends with today. Quitting softball was necessary to get where I am now."

When do you share this quitting story with others?

"I think it mainly comes up when people throw me something, like a set of keys. I catch it, and they are impressed."

What if you hadn't quit?

"I would have been angry and emotionally messy. Maybe I wouldn't have been able to handle my academic life. All teenagers can be irritable, but I would have been even more so. I wonder if I would self-sabotage and lose games on purpose. I think it would have damaged my status and my family's reputation."

What tradeoffs did you accept by quitting?

"Popularity. Theatre kids are not popular. And my parents' reputation, a little bit."

What does this quitting story say about you?

"It shows that I have the capacity to do one hundred and eighty degree turns really well… that if I really need to do something, I just do it."

What makes you most proud of your quitting story?

"I'm proud that I didn't grandstand it. That I didn't throw a fit, I didn't leave talking shit about the other girls, I still said 'hi' to them afterward even if some of them didn't say 'hi' back. I'm glad that I left with dignity. In other family situations I could be more volatile, but this decision was just so matter of fact. It laid a foundation for how I made decisions later in my life and let my family know about my choices."

What values does this quitting story say you have?

"It says that I value being authentic and keeping myself as real as possible. I was very honest with myself."

"I wasn't willing to put up with _____."

"I wasn't willing to put up with sacrificing my happiness for an ambiguous game."

I Quit Trying to Date Men

———

For Devon, their perspective on quitting things was always inextricably tied to having attention- deficit/hyperactivity disorder (ADHD) growing up.

"I would just lose patience with things," they say, forgiveness in their voice. "When I was a kid, I quit violin, piano, and guitar, each after only one year of pursuing them. Devon laughs when they think how they might have been really good at those instruments now if they hadn't quit. "But then, I just think that the reason I quit doing those things was because I simply wasn't enjoying them. So, I go back and forth a bit on what I think about quitting."

Devon, a native of New England, ties the shame Western culture places on quitting to the Puritan work ethic that is so deeply enshrined in everything we do.

I was in college when I first observed all of the lovely social welfare benefits and thirty-hour work weeks and vacation days and (at that time) well-funded public transportation our Enlightenment brothers and sisters in Europe enjoyed. I quickly formed the opinion that America would have been better off if we (or rather, Indigenous peoples) had followed in Europe's footsteps and oppressed those Pilgrims out of here the second their pious buckled boots had touched Plymouth Rock. WASPs go home! But leave your gin. That, I like.

"We tend to assume that if something isn't hard, then it's not good for us," Devon says, summing up a significant outcome of the Puritan work ethic. "Sometimes that may be true, sometimes a real struggle can make you appreciate things more and can make you better at things, but that's not always the case."

Devon brings up two specific areas where the Puritan work ethic can just plain suck and get in the way of making life decisions: work and relationships.

"I went through a rough period after graduate school where I had lots of different jobs in almost as many different cities. Several of the jobs I quit, I left because I had abusive bosses. A lot of people in my life at that time were like, 'Yeah, that's fucked up, but that's just how it goes, you know.'"

I recognize this fatalism. It's rampant in my own South Asian culture, where you constantly hear, "Tsk. What can you do?" in a wistful, rhetorical tone to any misfortune, slight, or challenge. Every time I hear it, I want to scream at the top of my lungs: "You can at least try to do something!" The status quo has never been for me.

"There's this assumption," Devon says, "that something is more worthwhile if it's hard, if you have to fight for it."

It's perhaps no surprise that Devon also connects the Puritan work ethic to another anti-quitting, self-punishing paradigm: capitalism.

"To have any worth in our society, you have to participate in this capitalist structure. Your sense of worth comes from your ability to do well in a job, make money, and buy things."

Devon sees this same dynamic playing out in relationships as well.

"There is so much stigma in our culture around breaking up with people, too, and quitting relationships. I think the stigma is one of the ways we punish ourselves."

Devon came out as non-binary right around their fortieth birthday. Being on the older side when they came out meant that they became a part of an entirely new community they hadn't yet had access to as an adult. In their first couple of years in this community, they saw plenty of guilt around leaving relationships.

"I'm in this Facebook support group for later-in-life lesbians," they say. "So many of the other people in that group struggle with guilt over leaving their husbands. They fret over how he was such a great guy, and they built such a great life together, he didn't do anything wrong. To me, it seems like they have nothing to feel guilty about; the husbands didn't do anything wrong for the relationship not to work, it's not a judgment of their character."

It's understood that many of these lesbians probably spent years denying their true identities and fighting for their marriages to work; in essence, fighting against who they were in order to satisfy societal expectations.

"Once I saw it in this group of my friends, I started seeing it everywhere… this idea that any relationship that is worthwhile is something for which you should want to or have to fight."

With one divorce under my belt and counting, I wonder the same thing as Devon: can't we just believe ourselves worthy of things that come easily?

Devon's perspective on quitting work and relationships is also profoundly influenced by their parents.

"My dad has been a really good quitting model for me. He is very successful professionally but had a very circuitous route to get there. When I was a little kid, he was an EMT; I used to call ambulances 'Daddy Cars.'" They laugh remembering how damn cute this is, "He was great at it too; he was the steward of his local union and was being recruited into management. When I was four years old, he quit and took an unpaid internship at a radio station. He'd studied broadcasting in college and really wanted to make a go of a career in that field. He was thirty-nine! He took this great leap, and it ended up being a very positive move for him."

Devon also saw the ease with which their parents supported each other during times of transition like this.

"Obviously, my mom and dad had an amazing partnership, and they made it work. Growing up, I never for a moment thought they might ever get divorced. It was always like they were swimming upstream together and that they liked working on the hard things together and genuinely enjoyed each other's company. I think this is where I formed my view that things like successful relationships don't have to be hard."

Getting diagnosed with ADHD a couple of years after finishing graduate school and going on medication helped Devon quit more "strategically" than they did before. No more flying the coop purely out of impatience.

"I was in Seattle," they say, "and I wasn't loving my job and was thinking about applying to PhD programs. But now I was able to take a beat and think of alternatives to what I'd always done before, which was to just completely jump ship. Instead, I decided to just take a different job at the same organization and that really set me on the career path I'm on now. Staying in Seattle allowed me to find and be a part of this great community that I still love. I was able to think of a smaller change that made me happier."

To me, this is an example of a type of quit that can be a good choice at many moments: the pivot. Devon made a big choice but based on their goals and improved ability to think through the tradeoffs, they made an internal switch up instead of an irreparable, irretrievable quit.

For Devon, quitting stopped being a fight or flight reaction in which they usually chose "flight." They were able, with the help of a diagnosis and medication, to find an alternative style of quitting things.

This ability to find nuance in the midst of big life decisions served them well during the time they were re-examining their gender and sexuality. Before Devon even deduced that they were non-binary or a lesbian, they quit one thing definitively: trying to date men.

They were assigned female at birth, and so they were always thought of as a "girl" and expected to like boys.

"I didn't really have a lot of crushes," Devon says, "but I remember in kindergarten a friend saying she had a crush on this one boy and asking me who I have a crush on. I said I didn't have a crush on anyone and her reaction was, 'Well, you have to have a crush on somebody!'" So I just pointed at a random boy and said I had a crush on him. And that's pretty much how I did crushes. Every year I'd just randomly choose a different boy. I thought that was just how it worked!"

Even though I am a cisgender, heterosexual female, I totally get this! I was a total late bloomer when it came to dating and boys, but I still wasn't as debilitatingly *thirsty* as a lot of my girlfriends seemed to be growing up. I remember being at one of the few popular-girl slumber parties I was invited to an elementary school and some Taylor or Monica or

Heather pouting that she didn't have any boy that she liked right then. "I need to have someone to like!" she groaned. Even if my loins were burning as eagerly as the hair on my upper lip was growing, my mind-only reaction was, "What the hell? Can't you just go through a day or week without crushing on a boy?"

I was lucky, though. I was straight, so I didn't need to pretend like Devon did. I was also a brown girl in a rural Ohio town, so I was never going to get laid anyway if we're honest.

Throughout high school and even college, Devon chalked up their admiration for women to objective social standards: women are the ones sexualized, so they are just more beautiful than men are.

Give me the choice of gazing at a naked man's body or a naked woman's body, and I'll always choose looking at a woman. Men just look so half-finished, like God decided to take a nap after finishing the upper body and got distracted by making mountains or whatever after he woke up. It's interesting to hear Devon chalk their appreciation for women up to their being more sexualized than men. Perhaps my "women are just objectively more attractive" opinion isn't so objective after all and instead represents some internalized sexualization. God knows that when I check other women out, it's out of envy and never longing or lust.

"Even though I was developing stronger and stronger attractions to women," Devon recalls, "I still had such a strong self-identification with being straight. I just thought, 'Okay, maybe I just think girls are pretty, and that's it.'"

They continued to date men, but nothing developed into anything serious. When Devon turned thirty and decided to buckle down and get serious about dating, they went "full bore" into online dating.

"For a full year, I was going on a date almost every single week. It was a good experiment because I decided if I can have an interesting email exchange with a guy, then I'll go out with him, and if he doesn't end up being my type I won't worry about it. I got really good at the mechanics of dating. I had a very analytical approach to it, and because I was never attracted to any of the guys, it was easier to think of it as a science experiment."

Dozens of experimental dates with men later, Devon hadn't clicked with anyone. When they look back on it now, also having learned from others who have gone through the same journey, Devon laughs about how easy it is to have really high standards for people of the gender to which you are not attracted.

"It's easy to do that when you're not actually attracted to them. It's a sort of defense mechanism. I did have high standards, as everyone should, but I didn't have physical attraction short circuiting any of that stuff."

I envy Devon for never having the experience of lowering their standards for a man because hormones got in the way.

Soon after this one-year experiment in Seattle, Devon moved to Washington, DC for a different job in digital strategy and tried to continue their man inquiry there.

"Dude...," they shake their head when asked about the men in DC. After more prodding: "DC has a very strong douchebag, bro vibe. I just saw too many guys with Redskins photos in their profiles, and I just couldn't imagine enjoying a conversation at a happy hour with them."

Even though I was all shacked up during the eight years I lived in DC, I have to vouch for what Devon says about the male dating pool there. I knew a lot of single men, and I adored them, but not once did I ever consider setting them up with a girlfriend of mine. I had a friend who even moved to New York just to find a better dating scene than DC.

The DC dating lab was closed very quickly, but Devon's time there was still instructive. While in DC, they started to have very obvious crushes on women and non-binary people. They also realized that they had stopped having crushes on men.

"I didn't really make the connection for myself at the time. I had just gotten so used to thinking of myself as mostly straight. I think there was also a part of me that was like, 'Oh man, it would be so embarrassing to come out at this age,'" they laugh. "It would be so embarrassing to have this thing that I didn't know about myself for forty years! Or maybe there was even a fear that people would think I had been lying all this time."

When they moved back to Seattle, a light bulb went off. They realized that they'd been telling themselves that they hadn't been attracted to anyone in a long time, but they had. To plenty of people. Just not to men.

A near-death experience provided them with even greater clarity about their identity.

"I went river tubing with a friend of mine, down a river we'd been on before. There were some rapids, and there was this tree in the water that had fallen down, and I got caught in it. I almost drowned. Two nights later, I woke up in the middle of the night and just told myself: you need to start dating women."

But the creeping doubt and the connection to their straight identity, however false, wedged its way back in.

"It's hard to explain, but I spent a lot of time thinking that I might be making this up, or I'm making excuses for why things haven't worked out between me and any of the guys I've dated."

Analysis came back in as well. Percentages even.

"I figured I was at least fifty percent attracted to men, so I guess that's who I should end up with."

My heart breaks for Devon as I hear the months of see-sawing that happened before they came to understand themselves more fully.

"Straight, cis people don't understand or see the long back and forth that a lot of gay or queer people go through before actually coming out. Ninety-five percent of our culture tells you that you're supposed to be straight. To go against that takes a lot of self-knowledge."

I've personally experienced and observed in others, this cor-
relation between self-knowledge and self-awareness and the
confidence it takes to quit something. The more you know
about yourself, your values, and what you are about, the more
you can quit without regret.

Not knowing their gender identity and dating preferences
was the missing piece for Devon, and it frustrated them.

"A big part of me was also like, 'Shouldn't I already know?'
We have this 'born this way' idea when it comes to queer-
ness, and so I thought if I wasn't sure then maybe I was
making it up."

For Devon, it wasn't trying to figure out if they were interested in women, this was undeniable. It was more about figuring out if they were interested in men. They spent a lot of
time pondering this question, trying to find an answer, and
reflecting deeply with the help of others.

Then, they suddenly stopped.

"I thought. 'Wait… why does this even matter?' I was pin-
ning so much of my understanding of my sexual orien-
tation on whether or not I was interested in men, which
was the only thing I wasn't sure about. That was the only
question mark."

Devon took a look at all the effort they'd put into running
their experiments with dating men in multiple cities and
finally decided: what does it matter if they like men or
don't?

Important primal scream at the patriarchy side note:
MEN TAKE UP SO MUCH FUCKING MENTAL ENERGY
EVEN WHEN YOU WANT NOTHING TO DO WITH
THEM!

They also had some inspiration from a married friend who, though she identifies as bisexual, hadn't dated men since her early twenties. She put it to Devon pretty simply: "I just decided that I don't want to date men. So, I don't."

This was a game changer for Devon and provided the clarity they needed.

"When I finally gave myself permission to never go on a date with a man ever again, it was such a profound sense of relief."

As someone who finalized their divorce during a global pandemic that required everyone to limit contact with others, I know this sense of relief so well. During a health crisis that requires physical distancing, no one is bothering me about if or when I'll get back out there and start dating! I can just hide out in my home and relive my "never going to get laid" glory days of my youth.

The relief Devon got by quitting trying to date men also brought greater confidence.

"It helped me feel more competent. I was able to take the space I needed, identify myself as queer, and acknowledge that I'm still figuring out a lot about myself. I do know that I want to be dating women. Once I decided to stop dating men, I was able to start coming out."

Their decision to quit what they once thought was an important part of their identity also helped them re-examine their perspective on failure.

"I saw this quote once that said something to the effect of it's okay to fail at things. Sometimes when you fail at something, it's because it wasn't right for you. I think about that a lot because when I was trying to date men, I often felt like a failure. I felt I was bad at dating, at relationships, or at intimacy. I've had to rewrite that narrative in my mind and tell myself that I didn't fail at something, I was actually very good at protecting myself from something that wasn't right for me."

Devon's decision to quit dating men definitely places them in a non-majority part of American culture.

"The biggest tradeoff I've had is giving up on hetero privilege. Giving up on that socially- and still governmentally sanctioned way of living. I had to tell my mom who I want to have sex with. That fucking sucks!"

It occurs to me that the only time I've ever had to assert my sexuality to my mom was in college when she politely asked me if I'd prefer she "find" me a girl instead of a boy. This is how un-laid I was. My own mother thought the only reason for my lack of boyfriends by age twenty was that I wanted a girlfriend instead. We straight people have it so easy.

Devon's process of coming to understand themself hasn't been all unicorns and rainbows. Taking on several marginalized identities halfway through their life has been "really weird" and resulted in them de-prioritizing their career for a bit while they figured themselves out.

They've also noticed a disconnect occurring between friends and family they developed relationships with when they thought they were straight.

"With any minority group," they explain, "there is going to be a different way of talking and relating within that group than you have with the majority group."

It's an imperfect comparison, but I think about what it would be like if my South Asian parents all of a sudden learned I am not also South Asian. We would lose so much of the common identity and experience that binds us.

"And I also think about how, if Trump wins again this year and we find ourselves in an even more fascistic society, I'm vulnerable in a way that I wouldn't have been five years ago."

They echo a sentiment felt by many. I've never felt more conspicuous, more dangerously exposed by the way I look than I did on November 9, 2016.

Luckily, I am revising this chapter on the eve of Joe Biden's inauguration. I know both Devon and I can't wait until morning.

* * *

Any regrets?

"I wish I hadn't taken so long and wasted so much time thinking I was mostly straight. I blame our culture, not myself. I wish I could go back to nineteen-year-old me and tell them to just give it more thought, spend some more time on this question."

What if you hadn't quit?

"If I hadn't quit dating men, I'm sure I'd still be stuck in that never-ending cycle of 'Oh, I'll start dating again in three months… another three months… now's not the right time.' I'm sure I'd be pretty depressed."

"Deciding to stop dating men is what enabled me to come out as queer and build a queer community. Having this community, especially during COVID, has just been so amazing for me and given me so much. It unlocked this whole area of changes that I needed."

What does this quitting story say about you?

"I believe that my happiness is important. I'm open to learning new things, even if it's about myself, and I'm really committed to being in good relationships with the people that I have in my life."

What makes you most proud of your quitting story?

"I'm really proud of myself for giving myself permission to say, 'If you don't want to do it, you don't have to do it.' I wish

I had done it earlier, but I'm proud that I eventually did. It hadn't even occurred to me that I needed permission to stop dating men, but as soon as it did, I did it."

"I feel like the past few years have been about me finding the end of this thread, and I just keep pulling at it and discovering all these wonderful things about myself, and it's brought so many great things into my life. I'm proud that I had the courage to authentically embrace all these new things I learned about myself."

"I wasn't willing to put up with _____."

"I wasn't willing to put up with forcing myself to go on dates that I was dreading, going through the motions with men I wasn't attracted to, and beating myself up about it."

I Quit Being a "Good Little Black Girl"

———

Trigger Warning: child sexual abuse,
racism, white supremacy

Lindsey's early feelings toward quitting are typical of perfectionists everywhere: quitting equals failing.

"When I was younger," she says, "I would have said the idea of quitting, or more specifically failing, would cause me to vomit in my mouth."

She attributes this to growing up in legacy American culture (hello Puritanism!), but also to her status as the daughter of first generation African American wealth.

"You learn very early on that we do not quit. We exceed. In order to be considered on par with our white contemporaries, we have to be the best."

This pressure to exceed expectations didn't just impact Lindsey's outward self, and it didn't merely influence her desire to be good at school or to excel in extracurriculars. It defined how she would value herself as a human being.

"I took on the idea very early in life, that what made me valuable and what made me lovable were all of the ways that I succeeded and achieved, and how I presented a perfect image of what it meant to be a good little Black girl in American society."

When Lindsey experienced sexual abuse as a young girl, it was all too easy for her abuser to convince her that her parents would stop loving her if she told them about the abuse. She tenderly speaks of the child version of herself in third person, a tried-and-true way to process complex emotions.

"Out of that little Lindsey, the tiny ego of a child is trying to make sense of what happened. The little child looks around and thinks 'Hm... if they can stop loving me for this, that must mean love is conditional." Lindsey continues to explain the tragic logic of a young, molested girl. "And if love is conditional, then I have to do everything to earn love and attention and to be valuable. And so, you can see how the child and trying to make sense of this, to fail or to quit would be equated with no longer being worthy of attention or love."

Her upbringing, often the only Black person in affluent spaces, is both similar and dissimilar to mine as the only Brown person among white people.

They were different in that, while most white people expected or at least were not surprised that my family was upper-middle class, Lindsey's white peers were often taken aback by how her affluence exceeded their expectations.

"I often contended with my white peers being surprised that my parents were wealthy and sometimes even wealthier than they were. That cognitive dissonance for these white children, it was not what they had been told the world was meant to look like; it was not what they saw on *COPS*."

Lindsey, now an anti-racism educator, researcher, and speaker, describes this "code switching" or "double consciousness" as "being told that you are not the norm, while having to identify oneself, and continually attempt to contend with the dominance of the oppressive culture. You are conditioned to be nice. Not to hold others accountable."

And Lindsey was rewarded for being "nice." She recalls a time in high school when her white, male basketball coach made tenth grade a "living hell" for her. She was often the subject of his irrational tirades, including one very alarming moment when he yelled at her across the court in front of the entire team and school. Lindsey unequivocally calls his behavior racist and patriarchal.

"One of the teachers—they might have also been the principal or head of the athletic department—came to me during that year and said that I should be so proud of how I was handling the situation. It was a Christian school. They said that God would be so proud of me. But there was never any mention of doing anything about this racism or this behavior. It was just 'good job for keeping quiet and shouldering all of this.'"

It's very easy to lose the ability to advocate for yourself if you are only ever rewarded for not doing so. Our experiences were similar in how one of us represents all of us.

"We ask little Black boys, little Black girls, little indigenous and other BIPOC children, immigrant children, and anybody that is the first of a generation that's trying to break through a class system to be perfect, to be representatives of the group that they now represent."

I suddenly realize that the awful term "Model Minority" and the cultural and familial pressures for perfection it conveys isn't the exclusive province of immigrants, let alone Asian immigrants. Lindsey, a Black American woman, experienced the same pressure to conform and to represent "her people" well, simply because of her proximity and access to whiteness. It makes me feel that, instead of Indian American, South Asian, first generation, or daughter of immigrants, the primary identity America wants me to have is the same it wants for Lindsey: not white.

I, like Lindsey, grew up with the message of "assimilate to be safe." Assimilate so you can (hopefully) not draw attention to your difference, but you must also be the best. This messaging is filthy with contradictions: to be the best is to be separate, distinct, to stand out. This is the opposite of assimilation. Unless you are white-presenting, white culture doesn't allow you to assimilate, to be a wallflower, to blend into the background. Visually, you will always stand out. The true message is clearer and easier to pursue if not to attain. You cannot fail... because we will all be judged based on your actions.

This did a number on Lindsey's sense of self.

"I didn't get to just be Lindsey, I had to be Lindsey as representing all of [white people's] racialized experiences with Black humans."

A big part of that representation meant there was little to no room for error. And what is one of the clearest ways to let the world know you made a mistake? Quitting. For Lindsey, not being the "good little Black girl" was to fail and be a failure.

The path Lindsey took to go from "quitting is failing" to quitting being a "good little Black girl" took some time. There wasn't some "big quit" or "I'm mad as hell and I'm not going to take it anymore!" moment.[5] Her journey to rethinking and reframing quitting and failure for herself began when she started out as a researcher when she was studying women and health. She began to look into what changes when women are centered in the health paradigm instead of cis, heteronormative, white men.

This inquiry led her to learn about how the socialization of patriarchy and misogyny culture has led to a system in which women are not allowed to fail or quit.

---

5   *Network*, directed by Sidney Lumet (Metro-Goldwyn-Mayer (MGM) 27 November 1976)

"In that research, I found the most socially liberated women were those who had adjusted their view of quitting, or of failure, and began to recognize failure as a stepping stone or a path to learning. Each failure taught them something about themselves."

This research influenced Lindsey's play, "Enlightened as Fuck," in which the trope of the "crazy woman" archetype is explored.

"The story of the 'crazy woman' is that she managed to exist outside the boundaries of patriarchal culture. She gets othered as too loud, too crazy, too eccentric, too dramatic, too bitchy, and all the things. But it was because she begins to step out of this white, Protestant, patriarchal, colonizer lens and says, 'I'm not going to play this game anymore. The system is stacked and unhealthy, and it has overcompensated toward one side without any balance.'"

The lesson for Lindsey is as clear as a WASP's family crystal: "The obsession with the fear of quitting or failing is actually a construct. It's not real."

Lindsey hints at something that I hadn't yet pondered: reframing quitting—failure and patriarchy along with it— has the power to be revolutionary for society.

Quitting absolutely revolutionized my own life. Once I got used to the idea that being a goody-two-shoes-perfectionist-do-all-the-right-things-that-other-people-are-saying-are-the-right-things was going to get me nowhere, I got comfortable with quitting fast. I looked at my life experiences, especially jobs, as experiments through which I could learn more about myself and what it was that I wanted in this world. Without knowing it or seeking it, I became one of those "socially liberated women" in Lindsey's research. I found what I wanted much faster than I would have if I had just bobbed along in obedience to the status quo. It's made me unafraid to make big personal (getting divorced) and professional (starting my own company) choices. Was this the path my immigrant parents anticipated for their high-achieving daughter? Probably not, but dashing expectations has always been worth it.

Lindsey's research also led her to look back on her earlier career as a professional contemporary dancer in a new light. That experience demanded a lot of failure only for her to get back up and do it again and again. The show must go on even if you fail. It cannot stop even if you have broken toes.

Sometimes our capacity to endure failure is much larger than we know.

All of Lindsey's research and reflection led to this conclusion: "The continual drive for perfection and the avoidance of discomfort are attributes of white supremacy culture," she says. "To be perfect suggests that one does not fail. And even when we do fail, we have this wonderful habit of calling it the 'reframe.' We always note some lesson we took away from it. We have been psychologically conditioned in the Western model to evade and avoid failure at every cost. We cannot just sit in our failure and allow it to consume us."

The women she had researched who were socially liberated through quitting had also learned not to be afraid to sit in their failures.

"The manifestation of the white deity and of white supremacy culture is very binary. You are either right or you're wrong. You are either good or you are bad. We, as a culture, do not understand that life exists in the gray. And so, we become obsessed with avoiding failure and avoiding quitting, and we convince little children that to quit or to fail is a mark on your character as opposed to a mark in your action. You *are* a quitter. You *are* failure."

Lindsey's first expression of no longer being the "good little Black girl" was when she decided to quit the holistic health business she was running in Australia. It wasn't profitable. Her friend and accountant told her that she was, in effect, running a charity, not a business. Lindsey had also just given birth to her daughter, and her focus was on her child.

As someone who has run her own company for seven years, I know the feeling of having your work so inextricably tied to your identity.

"It was not necessarily that I had failed at the company, it was that I was being *seen* to fail, that I was being *seen* to quit. You couldn't have convinced me that death was more painful because, subconsciously, the ego is telling you all these people in your life are going to leave you now that you failed. The truth is going to come out."

Lindsey's ongoing journey has included recognizing that she had been doing what was expected of her instead of living her own life.

"I had spent so much of my life playing the character: always nice, always kind, always thoughtful, always accommodating. All while struggling with my true self, which is that 'crazy,' too much, too loud woman. But sometimes I am that, and sometimes, I am this. We are all contradictions."

And, even once she recognized the dissonance and the need for change, she found that transforming this attitude wasn't easy. She had her fair share of desperately trying to stick with the status quo.

"The work that it took me to dismantle all of that: divorce, recreating the relationship with my parents, letting friends go… I would say that I understand why people don't do it. Brené Brown calls it 'surviving the wilderness.' When we have very few examples of what the alternative would look like, it often seems safer to just stick with the status quo."

"There was a time when I said to myself, 'Okay, now you're a mom, and you should do the things that moms do, like have a regular job. And I'd try job after job and just quit all of them because they were so soul sucking. For somebody else, these might have been dream jobs. Far be it for me to hold a space and keep them from it."

Here we see, again, that there can be generosity in the act of quitting.

Even as she continued to unpack America's history and her own upbringing and desire to be the "good little Black girl," she occasionally found herself caught in the same pattern of her "niceness," suppressing her true self.

There was a moment when she got a "regular job" as a project manager at an organization she was incredibly excited about. Not only was the CEO a woman, but so were most of the upper management and staff. The team she happened to be assigned to was co-led by two older white men; both had previously been executives at other organizations.

"They just could not fathom how this young Black girl got brought in to be their project manager," Lindsey says.

In the first meeting, the two men snidely asked Lindsey how a dancer becomes an entrepreneur and a project manager. Just as in the aftermath of her experience with her school basketball coach, Lindsey was congratulated by her leaders for putting up with it.

Despite disappointing experiences like being rewarded for playing the character of "good little Black girl," Lindsey didn't stop further examining who she really was and where she fit within the story of America. She continued to heal from her childhood trauma and listened to the stories of healing that others had to share to help her interpret her own. "The history of America is un-dealt with trauma," she says. But Lindsey was committed to dealing with her own.

"It became more and more clear that I was still playing this character of Lindsey. I had to start to unravel, 'What is this character and what is actually you, Lindsey?' For example, how did I end up with a husband who doesn't want to accept that misogyny and racism exist, let alone accept that he is complicit in it? Why is it that I can't express my true self around my parents?"

Lindsey has spent a lot of time doing this unraveling and digging deeper into her true, not-so-good little Black girl self. She paraphrases Viktor Frankl: "Between stimulus and response, there is space. And in that space is the opportunity to choose one's actions. A lot of my personal practice and work with communities is to keep expanding that space. And within that space to do what Dr. Cornel West calls constant self-interrogation."

Lindsey's personal work and self-interrogation have led her to try to be more, and less, of certain things: less of a rescuer of others; more saying "no"; less trying to be the entertainer when around her friends; more dressing for herself rather than to be seen; less performative mothering to be seen by others as a good mother.

She was recently confronted with a situation that she handled very differently because of the personal work she's done. A client, upon realizing that they had systemic racism at the root of their organization, wanted to bail on a contract for anti-racism work they had signed with Lindsey's company.

"In the past I would have waffled. But now, I was like, 'Call the lawyer. Here's the paper you signed.'"

To be a "good little Black girl" is inherently relying on a value created outside of yourself. It's others who are defining what it means to be "good." It's a way to live your life for others instead of yourself. And Lindsey is done with all that.

Her quitting story is a constant, ongoing one; she is continually in the act of quitting the good little Black girl she was conditioned to be.

"Failure is something that I've learned to embrace as one integral part of the human experience. It's one million tiny decisions I make every day."

* * *

Any regrets?

"No."

Who has been influential to your quitting story?

"My children. My daughter, especially, models what it's like to not be a 'good little Black girl.' A man on the street once pulled that thing of asking her to smile, and she immediately responded "Why?" She's only four! She exhibits self-awareness and internal strength. I feel like I need to model that same behavior, so she doesn't have to question that strength or dampen it in any way. I've realized that some of the tactics and tools I used to play a character are not beneficial to me, and they aren't beneficial to my children.

What tradeoffs did you accept by quitting?

"Will I ever find partnership in somebody who's not asking me to be less than I am? I don't know the answer yet."

"I've learned to scrutinize my friendships more and evaluate where I was cast as the 'Black' friend. Some friendships needed to transition out so that others could transition in."

What makes you most proud of your quitting story?

"That I'm a Black woman. Right now, we are living in a great exodus of Black women from the 'good little Black girl' banner, and in this might be how we save our humanity."

What values does this quitting story say you have?

"Determination, grace, creativity, flexibility, and agility. Pretty much the traits of a professional dancer!"

"I wasn't willing to put up with _____."

"I wasn't willing to put up with not reaching my highest potential."

QUITTING
ASPIRATIONS

I Quit Graduate School

It's not that Elly never quit things growing up… it's that she only quit things when she just couldn't handle them anymore.

"There was one year in middle school when I was playing three different sports in one season," she says, shaking her head. "After school, I'd go from track practice to soccer practice to basketball practice. It was insane."

No parent or coach or sibling was pushing Elly to do all this. She was just a naturally motivated, interested, goal-oriented person at a young age. She genuinely wanted to do all of the things.

"I really wanted to do it all. But eventually, the writing was on the wall, and I couldn't do all of them. So, I quit track since that was my least favorite of the three. And then I eventually quit basketball, which was a harder decision because I think I could have played varsity in high school."

But her passion was soccer, and she had the goal of playing it in college. So, she narrowed her sports focus to that.

In high school, she stayed focused on her soccer goals. Her senior year, she hurt her knee playing and had to have surgery. It was a very stressful time for someone like Elly, who was accustomed to doing it all. She was trying to excel in all her Advanced Placement (AP) classes, doing all the same clubs, while also adding in the time pressure of physical therapy.

It was Elly's mom who gently reminded her that her life didn't have to be full of so much achievement-related stress.

"My mom sat me down and said, 'You know, it's okay to get a B. You don't have to do it all.' It was very freeing, and I think having that happen to me at a younger age was really fortunate."

As you might have guessed, Elly didn't excel in just sports. She's one of those people who was good in all her subjects, which can sometimes be hard because there's no obvious path to choose. I, on the other hand, had to try really hard to get B-pluses in most of my high school math and science classes, but the humanities and social sciences came much more naturally. I never once considered going into a STEM field. But Elly? She was torn.

"I was good at math and science, but I didn't really want to go the doctor or engineer route," she says. "I am super squeamish, and I don't think I was left-brained enough for engineering. We had a family friend who was a speech pathologist, and that seemed medical adjacent enough without being gross."

From chatting with this family friend, she was convinced that she'd enjoy speech pathology. She found a liberal arts college that had both a Division III soccer team and a program that included a speech pathology major. This was rare, considering how specialized the degree is. Everything was shaping up nicely for Elly.

Undergrad was an enjoyable breeze, too.

"I had this one professor who was a freaking genius," she remembers. "He made *ears* interesting!"

Along the way, she realized that she was more interested in the field of audiology because it fit her left-brained-ness better.

"Speech pathology was like, 'We don't really know what causes stuttering, so let's try this therapy...and then THIS therapy.' I was like, 'No, let me diagnose your hearing loss and let's fix this.'"

Her senior year of college, everything crystallized in her year-long capstone research project.

"I realized that, as a soccer player, when you're on the field you are talking and communicating and shouting to everybody to help us play better. I was curious: how do deaf people do that? My thesis was on communication styles and tactics of deaf and hard of hearing collegiate athletes."

Elly learned a lot about Deaf culture and the history of audiology. She didn't like what she learned, which included a time in history when audiologists forced deaf people to talk and forced them to hear. There was also a period in which deaf people were slapped on the hands if they used sign language. This unsettled Elly.

She also learned that in today's Deaf culture, audiology is still controversial.

"They call it Deaf—capital D—" she explains, "to signal that they are very proud to be deaf and that American Sign Language is their first language. I'm learning that one opinion is that cochlear implants are considered genocide for those who are proud to be deaf. The sign for 'cochlear implant' is something like 'devil of the head.'"

Not only that but for a deaf child to be able to develop fluent spoken English, a cochlear implant needs to be implanted by the time they are six months old when language starts to develop.

"Many in the Deaf community feel that people should wait and be able to make that decision as an adult. But they are never going to develop speech at that point. It's a very complicated thing to weigh."

The injustices that audiology was founded on and its perceptions in current Deaf culture gave Elly pause: after nearly four years of devotion to it, was this really a field that she wanted to go into?

Pivoting and changing majors wasn't an option.

"This was a pretty expensive, private school," she says. "It was very much a four years and you're done situation."

She was stuck between a rock and hard place: finish a degree that set her up for a very specialized profession that she was having serious doubts about? Or... what? The sunk costs were, well, sunk.

It's this kind of sunk cost fallacy thinking that features so prominently in a lot of (mis)calculations when it comes to quitting. It's another trick we play on ourselves that prevents us from making big, important decisions when we know we need them.

It was the middle of her senior year, so Elly had to make some sort of move.

"I was needing to apply to graduate school because you can't really be an audiologist without a doctorate." Here, Elly was living the economic theory of path dependence, which can be summed up this way: the decisions presented to people are dependent on previous decisions or experiences made in the past. She'd invented a false belief that because she had studied audiology in undergrad (a prior decision), she had to continue with it (it's the only available decision, even though she had grave concerns about it).

Her college gave her funding for her capstone project so she could go to Washington, DC, and do additional research at Gallaudet University, which educates deaf and hard-of-hearing students.

While there, Elly observed various sports, including volleyball and basketball. She took notes and interviewed the athletes. Her time at Gallaudet made her decide to pursue her doctorate.

"After learning what I did about audiology, Gallaudet was the only place I would consider going. Interestingly, they do have an audiology program. It's probably the one program at the university where everybody is hearing."

Most other graduate audiology programs view being deaf or hard of hearing as a disability. Elly was attracted to Gallaudet because it viewed it as a communications barrier, and they had more respect for Deaf culture.

"They were more about giving [Deaf people] options to choose what's right for you, rather than saying your child should get cochlear implants or should be wearing hearing aids."

Because she had done very well in undergrad, she got accepted to Gallaudet's audiology doctorate program.

"This is where luck comes in," she says.

Elly had grown up in Ohio, but just as she was about to graduate college, her dad got a new job in the Washington, DC, area. Ten days after her graduation, she and her parents moved to Northern Virginia together. This good fortune comes into play later.

Despite the slight stumble around if audiology was right for her or not, the universe was aligning all its stars for Elly to keep following this path.

In the summer before she started graduate school, she got an internship at a hospital center doing hearing screenings on newborn babies, the exact right experience for a budding audiologist to get.

She hated it.

"It was the most boring job. Literally, all I would do is go up to a newborn baby as they're asleep and put a little thing in their ear and push a button and mark down what the reading said. I had to learn how to swaddle a baby because you have to get them to fall asleep first. I'm not a baby person to begin with!"

Boredom aside, I have to imagine this also felt to Elly like the first step toward an infant having the choice of cochlear implant made for them. She acknowledges that internships are supposed to be pretty basic and boring, but she also found herself being utterly disinterested in anything she saw the audiologists, speech pathologists, or medical doctors around her were doing.

Ever accepting of her current circumstances, she looked at what else she might be able to do.

"There was one other option. I could, instead of doing pediatric audiology, work with older people... but that would just be turning dials on hearing aids."

Even the process of making hearing aids met the "gross" factor of medical work that Elly knew she always wanted to avoid: if you mess up the earmold, there's a risk of tearing someone's eardrum out.

"I just wasn't finding anything. In undergrad, I had really enjoyed studying the ear at the theoretical level. But once I got into the practice of it, it just wasn't my thing."

I feel the unfairness of this. Elly had dedicated years of her young life to studying a highly specialized profession. The moment she started practicing it, however, she realized it wasn't for her. She received new information that she had little way of learning earlier, and she now had to decide if she'd use that new information to make a change.

It was just halfway through the first semester, and she was already unhappy. She went to her parent's house in Virginia nearly every weekend, trying to get some distance from the source of her joylessness.

Just like in middle school, it was her mom who helped her see that there were more options available to her than she thought.

"She listened to what I was struggling with, and she suggested that I get into the field of conflict resolution, because I was struggling with these conflicts that existed between these opposing camps in the treatment of people who are deaf. She reminded me that I've always been a harmonious person. She also outright said that I was miserable, and she wasn't used to seeing me like that."

Once again, Elly's mom lifted the veil for her and reminded her that she had agency.

"It was like she gave me that permission: 'I don't have to do this.'"

I think of myself as a fairly self-aware person, but it never ceases to amaze me how often others see things in me long before I discover them. I thought I became an atheist late in high school; my best friend since second grade says she always knew that I was an atheist. When I told my friends in high school that I was headed to New York City for college, most of them responded with, "We could have told you that when we were in elementary school." When I was ready to quit my corporate consulting job and start my own company, I told my friends that I had recently realized that I just wasn't that "typical" South Asian who could blindly obey authority and respect bureaucracy; their reaction was the equivalent of "No shit, Sherlock."

Sometimes we are surprises only to ourselves.

Elly didn't go into conflict resolution like her mom suggested, but seeing an example of another option in the world gave Elly hope. She ultimately wended her way into business consulting and leadership training.

Elly quit halfway through her first semester, but it took a while for the Band-Aid to be ripped off.

"I knew at some point in my life I was probably going to go to grad school for something," she justifies. "So, I decided to finish out the semester just so it wouldn't look like I couldn't cut it in another graduate program. It was important to me that I finish it out so I could set myself up better for later on."

She got a 4.0 that semester. Of course, she did! She knew that what she was about to quit still had a role to play in what she was moving toward.

"It was like I could breathe again," she says about quitting graduate school. Like so many quitters, by decisively making a big choice to move away from something that was no longer serving her, Elly found a whole new world of opportunity that she couldn't have expected.

"I have an MBA now, and I never ever would have thought I would do that. My dad worked for the government and my mom worked in nonprofits; so, I grew up assuming business was evil and greedy. But the first job I found after quitting graduate school was with a small woman-owned company that focused on health and human services government contracts. I wouldn't have realized that business can be ethical and good. I went to business school and joined clubs there, so first I found improv and sketch comedy and then I found weekend film festivals, which are still a huge part of my life. Improv changed my personality so much and gave me so much confidence; it made me a better consultant and it got me a job where I am now doing a lot of training and speaking in front of people."

Elly's story shows how powerful quitting can be as a means for reinvention. Quitting is too often associated with failure or being stuck. But Elly used increased knowledge of both her original field of study and of herself to refine her choices and make better decisions.

She's grateful for her experience, and it's given her a fresh outlook on quitting.

"I think quitting is a way to put yourself in a better place. You're quitting something that is negative in your life in order to free up that space to do something positive for yourself. It can take a while to get to that point of realizing that 'no, this is bad for me.' And then, obviously, it is very scary if you don't have something lined up. I think that's probably why a lot of people hang on to things for so long because they're afraid of what might be next. In my opinion, you will never find that 'next' unless you take that leap, unless you end the thing that is harmful for you."

* * *

Any regrets?

"I don't think so. It was lucky my parents were also living in DC at that time. I was able to find a job within four months. That wouldn't have happened if I'd gone back to where I was from in Ohio."

"This story also shaped the way I think about my career going forward. I don't actually make plans anymore. I don't necessarily have career goals because the one time I had my life all mapped out, it blew up in my face. Now, I focus on doing well at whatever I'm working on and being open to other things that I maybe wouldn't have considered. I became more spontaneous."

What if you hadn't quit?

"I think I would have been pretty miserable. There is the chance that maybe I would have become less scared of doing the ear thing but..."

"Originally, I used to think, 'Oh, I would have made a lot of money as an audiologist. But you know, I make a lot of money now, just in a different way."

"I probably wouldn't have gotten involved in improv because I got into that in business school."

What is the story you tell yourself about this quitting experience?

"I was miserable, and I wanted to stop being miserable. It was risky, and I didn't really have a plan. But it was great, and it worked out."

What tradeoffs did you accept by quitting?

"Not having a plan. I had to work retail; I got a job at the Apple Store just before I quit. I had to live with my parents for about a year before I made enough money to move out."

"The biggest one was that uncertainty. Going from a very clear, 'I have the next four years of my life planned,' to 'now I don't even know what the next four months are going to look like.'"

What does this quitting story say about you?

"I think it was brave. I think I was sticking up for myself, I respect myself, and I respect my happiness. I wasn't going to accept being unhappy."

What makes you most proud of your quitting story?

"I was able to get where I am now through a different way. I ultimately wound up very successful with my career without ever even knowing that this type of career exists."

What values does this quitting story say you have?

"Self-respect is important. You shouldn't do something because you think you're supposed to. Drive, as well. Perseverance. Commitment when it came to finishing the semester."

"Being open to learning, growing, experiencing, and understanding that, as human beings, we change. Not only is that okay, but it's important."

"I wasn't willing to put up with _____."

"I wasn't willing to put up with crying every night."

"I wasn't willing to put up with doing something just because, at one point, I thought it was the thing I needed to do."

I Quit Trying to Become a Parent

Courtney never knew she wanted to have kids until she did. Like me, she didn't really plan her life out with children in mind.

"I was born and raised in LA. I was living in LA and working in the music business. I really imagined I'd have a life where I threw everything at my career and settled for dating D-list celebrities."

Marrying her husband, which she describes as the best decision she ever made, wasn't what changed her mind.

"The night I turned thirty, it was like my biological clock just turned on," she says.

While I would have snoozed that clock's alarm well past menopause, Courtney was awakened: she wanted to be a parent.

Courtney and her husband decided to start trying for a baby a year after they got married and moved to Nashville. The timing was right, in part, because Courtney had just quit her career in the music business, which was burning her out.

"I was like, if I get pregnant, I don't want to have this stressful job," she says. "I just wanted to find a job that I didn't have to be feel chained in by anymore. I wanted something that I enjoyed, and could leave at work at the end of the day."

The job she found just so happened to be a job at a yoga studio that focused primarily on prenatal and postnatal yoga. It was great for a while; she got to be around moms-to-be and new moms and their infants all day. Then she would go home and try to make a baby of her own with her husband.

"It was super fun in the beginning, I was like 'Oh I can't wait to be a mom just like the rest of them!'" She even got certified to teach kids yoga for eighteen-month to four-year-old.

It all stopped being fun after the first six months of trying to conceive the "natural" way. Despite Courtney's giddy excitement convincing her that she was pregnant every month, she wasn't. She had been diagnosed with polycystic ovary syndrome (PCOS), a condition that produces higher than normal amounts of male hormones and can make it harder to become pregnant at age fourteen. Courtney had six laparoscopies to treat it by the time she and her husband started trying to conceive.

"We knew it would be an uphill battle," she admits. "But when we started, it was so exciting, I felt so grown up to think that I was going to be somebody's mother."

Her excitement led to diligence. She saved all of her home pregnancy tests, taped them into a notebook with the date and time she took them. It might have been the earliest start to a baby book in history.

What she describes as her "wishful thinking" about how easy it would be to conceive came, in part, from what teenagers are told about sex and pregnancy.

"Your average person probably loses their virginity between the ages of eighteen to twenty-five," she explains. "So, you spend a solid ten years thinking that if you make one wrong move or look the wrong way, you're going to get pregnant. And then all of a sudden, you are making the moves that were once wrong and assuming you're going to get pregnant."

Hidden behind society's fears of teenage (women's) promiscuity is the assumption that it's always easy to get pregnant. Courtney would learn the hard way that this isn't the case.

The fun of trying started to wear off as the methods escalated in specificity and "unsexiness." She tracked her ovulation with various apps and by taking her temperature; then paid attention to her cervix opening and cervical mucus; took medication to force ovulation; and then... Googled. Desperate Internet searches led to Courtney trying a lot of old wives' tales, including eating "so many fucking pineapple cores and brazil nuts."

"I think I was in denial that I was going to have the issues that I did. So, I just decided to throw everything at it."

Throwing everything at something was in line with Courtney's character. She remembers writing a ridiculously long book report on Mozart in the fifth grade; it was supposed to be one-page, but hers clocked in at fifteen.

"I didn't know how to quit or stop," she reflects. "I didn't know when enough was enough. So, I just kept going." The stress of figuring out when to discard irrelevant information or knowing when something was "done" led to panic attacks.

Underlying all this is the societal assumption that "more is better." Try harder, work longer, earn more, succeed faster. These tropes that the best (or only) way to get what you want is to keep doing more are often what can prevent us from quitting when we should.

After more than a year without conception, it was time to go to the professionals. She took a test with her OB/GYN that involved pushing dye through her uterus, and her fallopian tubes were declared "fine." The fertility specialist who looked at the results, though, told Courtney that her tubes were blocked and would have to be unblocked if an egg were ever to make its way from her ovaries to her uterus.

"It was at this point that we realized this was going to be way bigger. The specialist recommended bypassing any methods to clear my tubes and instead go straight to in vitro fertilization." This would require Courtney's tubes to be removed entirely. Her tubes were so damaged and filled with fluid by the PCOS, scar tissue from the laparoscopies, endometriosis, and other uterine conditions, that the risk of a dangerous ectopic pregnancy was way too high. Doing IVF with her tubes intact increased the risk of the fluid damaging any embryo.

"Anything that can happen to a uterus happened to mine."

There was no way she could get pregnant with her tubes in that condition, but learning this had a surprising effect on Courtney.

"That was like the biggest sigh of relief, because when you try to get pregnant, your first thought is always, 'what am I doing wrong'? I wasn't doing anything wrong. It was like this weight off our shoulders that was like, 'holy crap, there is nothing we can do without medical intervention.'"

She had her fallopian tubes removed. Physically, it wasn't a big moment for Courtney, but the emotional toll was far greater.

"All of a sudden it was like, 'Holy shit, I am literally infertile at this point. I am 100 percent sterile without tubes.'" She likens her post-surgery reaction to every time she gets a new tattoo.

"I literally freak out for half an hour. Like, 'What did I do? Am I going to regret this?' Then I'm done, and it's good."

Courtney quickly got over what the surgery signified: "I was no more infertile than I was the day before my surgery." Having her tubes removed was a means to an end. Courtney and her husband got excited about being parents again.

"Every time you introduce a new intervention, whether it's a procedure or a vitamin, it gives you this renewed sense of hope." And there were plenty of procedures and tests to come before they even got to the IVF. Learning about the process convinced Courtney to not start graduate school that year because it would be too hard to handle doing both.

She had her uterus measured by something called a saline sonogram; genetic testing was done to avoid birth defects; medications were taken to stimulate ovary production and suppress hormone production; and her husband's sperm had to be paired with hamster eggs to see if they were capable of fertilization.

"Yeah, we called him 'Hamster Daddy' for a long time after that," she laughs.

Courtney recalls the hormone suppression doing a number on her; she cried in more than one doctor's waiting room and bawled at an episode of *Transparent* when a long-lost family turtle was found, and she couldn't handle how lonely it must have been.

During periods of hormone stimulation, Courtney underwent intensive monitoring to know when it was the right moment to retrieve her eggs. She went into the clinic every couple of days for ultrasounds and monitors and to get her hormones and follicles checked. When they thought Courtney was in the "sweet spot," they gave her an injection to force ovulation over the next thirty-six hours. At hour thirty-four, they retrieved them.

This retrieval was the beginning of the first of three IVF "cycles" Courtney would go through. She ultimately had ten embryos transferred to her uterus across six procedures. Ten embryos fertilized with her husband's sperm meant ten chances for a baby.

None of them implanted in Courtney's uterus, but the "more is better" instinct we all have kicked in; Courtney was ready to keep going and try more experimental methods. Her conservative fertility clinic in Nashville, however, was not. So, she and her husband found a fertility doctor in upstate New York.

"He is an out of his mind, crazy professor type. He tries everything," she says, fondly. They FedExed her embryos to him, and Courtney thought how fun it would be to have a "Baby's First FedEx" page in the baby book. They started flying back and forth from Nashville to New York.

Courtney started doing "all kinds of crazy, out-there things" with the doctor. She did intralipid drips that were a thousand dollars a pop and lasted seven hours. She did plasma treatments in her uterus. She did cancer drugs. Blood thinners. The now-infamous hydroxychloroquine.

"It was this weird badge of honor to have all these bags of used vials around the house," she says. They were evidence of her effort and never-give-up attitude.

She did three more transfer procedures with the New York doctor; the final one transferred four of her embryos. Throughout all this, she also had to have a couple of more laparoscopies for her PCOS and endometriosis.

The day before she learned that none of the four embryos had been implanted, she got into a car accident. They had been on their IVF journey for four years. It was time for a break.

Later that same year, it was time for another surgery, this time to try to confirm suspicions that Courtney had adeno-myosis. She describes adenomyosis as "when endometriosis grows backward into the walls of your uterus." It causes men-strual bleeding so heavy that Courtney considered wearing adult diapers to bed. She went to a different specialist this time, thinking she might be able to do something different for her or give her some new information that might mean IVF would work in the future. No such luck.

"She said I was going to need a hysterectomy."

But Courtney was undeterred and went back to a trusty weapon: Google. She spent the next month researching var-ious cures for adenomyosis. The only one she found was a hysterectomy, which would mean she'd never be able to be pregnant. But she also found something that gave her hope for keeping her uterus and continuing with IVF.

"I found this one surgery that literally only two people in the world do. They cut open your uterus, and they butterfly it open. They take out the inner layer of it to remove the adenomyosis. Then, they stitch your uterus back together in the hope that it will solidly fuse." She describes it with the same shock and awe that I felt while hearing this process.

This was the moment Courtney decided to quit trying to be a parent through fertility treatments.

"When I realized how seriously I was considering this surgery, I had this 'Oh my god, what am I doing?' moment. I couldn't do it anymore."

She went back to her OG/GYN and got a hysterectomy.

It's been a year since Courtney and her husband decided to stop trying to be parents, and she got a hysterectomy, which she describes as "incredible." She is still flabbergasted by the lengths she was willing to go to, those she almost went to, to have a baby.

"I get all of these memories back of posts I made on Instagram and Facebook at the time. I just stop sometimes and think 'Holy shit, what was I doing?' I never even considered 'what is this doing to my body?' Where would we find the money?' It didn't matter. If it gave me a baby, that was literally the only thing I cared about. I also know that I'm in an immense place of privilege that we were even able to go into the kind of debt we did."

Despite all of her efforts, traditional and experimental, a pregnancy never happened for them. Courtney has a lot to say about why she was willing to go so far as to keep trying.

"When it came to my body, I didn't care. I just kept going. I was really miserable. Every time it failed, I looked back and asked myself 'What did I do wrong?'"

One of the big things in the infertility world is this constant mantra and culture of "don't give up."

"Anyone and everyone you meet and share your challenges with will say 'Don't give up!' or "This will happen for you!' or 'I can tell you're supposed to be a mother!'" Courtney sounds exhausted just repeating a small handful of the well-meaning but toxically positive comments she's had to endure. "People can't just sit in the discomfort someone is sharing with them. They can't just say 'I'm sorry you are going through this' or 'What can I do to help?'" So instead, people in Courtney's position get an onslaught of misguided positive thinking platitudes.

This wasn't the first time Courtney had encountered this kind of toxic positivity. Earlier in her life, she had struggled with an eating disorder. The admiration and support she got for losing weight made it that much harder to quit.

"I had lost a hundred pounds in eight months. I was really sick," she says, sadly. "And nobody cares how it's being done. They just praise the fact that you're doing it, that you are losing weight."

I am certain I am guilty of doing this at times, of falling into the "ignorant cheerleader" role when faced with an experience to which I don't know how to react, but just because it's borne of ignorance or goodwill doesn't make it any less unbearable for the person going through that experience. In speaking with Courtney, I also realize how some of that toxic positivity is the only language we have available to us; we see it and hear it all over the place, especially in marketing.

The infertility world, much like the wellness world and anything else that is designed to profit off of women being dissatisfied with themselves, is a business.

"If you search infertility-anything, there's something that someone's figured out how to monetize," Courtney says. "You are told, 'Don't give up if you just keep doing this long enough, it's going to work.' And that's not necessarily true."

In the business of infertility, to say "this may not happen for you" is viewed as counterproductive negative thinking rather than a real, possible outcome.

For Courtney, the consistent refrain of "don't give up" turned into pressure not to disappoint others. For a long time, the screensaver on her phone had a quote on it to help her keep going: "You haven't come this far to only come this far."

"There is a huge misconception that quitting means you didn't want it as badly as everyone else." Courtney describes this as a "really shitty narrative" that results in people trying for longer than they truly want to try to get pregnant.

The unfairness of it all is brutal. The only sign that you wanted a baby "enough" in this logical dystopia is that the treatments worked, and you ended up with a baby. But you could have endured all the same treatments and life disruption as the person it worked for and still not have a baby as proof of your irrefutable desire. How are you supposed to prove that you wanted it just as badly? Why do you even have to do so? Absent a baby, the only way to show that you really want a baby is to keep enduring pain to avoid the scarlet letter that comes with giving up on other people's hopes for you. In other words, the only way Courtney could prove she wanted a baby was to not quit something she knew wasn't going to work for her.

"I see so many women who decide to be child-free getting judged for it," she says. "And it's the same in the infertility world; it's like, 'How dare you not do literally everything to have a child?'"

This can turn to pursue fertility treatments and alternatives into a bit of an addiction or a carnival ride you don't think you can get off without fearing the entire world will claim you don't like fun.

"I didn't even question things before I dumped some of this stuff in my body. 'Whatever, if there's a chance, fine.' I was willing to keep doing more, more, and more until I hit a wall. My body and brain told me I couldn't do it anymore."

The fear of missing out, or FOMO, is also at play.

"There's always that constant thought of, 'What if the next one works?' That makes it really hard to quit."

"No one lets you grieve before you quit. So, it's like this constant pressure to be positive, envision it, see it, and believe it will happen, which, for the record, only puts more stress on you.

The through-line to all this is very similar to other societal pressures to not quit. "If you want doesn't happen, it's 100 percent your fault." There are many things that we can will into existence by making strong choices and decisions in life... this book is chock full of examples. You cannot, however, make the choice for your body to bear a child. Some things are just out of your control. The only thing in your control is how you choose to react and respond to your circumstances.

"Where is the line between giving up and learning the answer to my question? At what point was I willing to accept that my answer was 'no'?"

Once Courtney and her husband felt they had their question answered definitively, they did explore other options to become parents. Surrogacy was something they just couldn't afford after spending so much time and so many resources on infertility treatments. Domestic infant adoption was something they just weren't comfortable with due to a mismatch between their values and the values so many US adoption agencies espouse. After seven years of heartbreak, they had to take into consideration where they were now; overall, they felt that they didn't want to start a family anymore, as they were nearing their forties.

"It wouldn't have been in the best interest of the child. We had to figure out the difference between benefitting ourselves and benefitting our potential child."

Courtney's quitting story is an interesting example of how a "good" quit doesn't always have to come because something violated your values. Nothing about Courtney's fertility journey transgressed who she was or what she stood for; she made a different choice based on the information she was getting from her efforts to become a parent.

This past fall, she started the social work graduate program she had delayed to do IVF. One reason why she chose social work is because her fertility journey has made her more passionate about reproductive rights and getting things like fertility treatments and abortions viewed as health care and covered by health insurance.

Starting graduate school was an incredibly meaningful milestone for Courtney.

"Grad school was the first thing I did that was for the advancement of myself and not in service of this fictional baby." She takes a breath, "I had to give up that fictional baby to start living for myself."

She learned the concept of looking at her life like a house being built while she was in therapy. For her, parenthood was always a part of the foundation of that house.

"I had to separate that, so that *I* was the foundation, and parenthood was just another part of the house."

The toxic positivity still crept into her life. She'd be told, again with good intentions, that she was just a "Mother without a child" or "You're a mama, anyway!"

"At a certain point, I had to just say, 'No, I'm not.'"

She hasn't simply gained the mental and emotional space to start graduate school. Quitting trying to become a parent also brought other benefits to her life.

"A lot of couples are torn apart by an experience like ours. I'm lucky that I've never had to worry about my marriage during all this, even though for much of our marriage we thought and talked of *nothing* else but this child that didn't exist. I can't tell you how many times I looked at him and told him that I'd totally understand if he left me for someone who could have children. I finally feel like we can just be a happy couple now and not have this cloud over our heads. We are stronger than ever."

They are currently planning a "giant trip" with all the credit card miles they earned from their failed IVF treatments. They also haven't lost their delightfully wicked sense of humor in imagining their child-free life ahead.

"We joke that, someday, we want to have this incredible house with lots of glass and lots of sharp edges, and that is near really unsafe water."

They have also set a goal of visiting one Michelin-starred restaurant every year.

She gets really excited when she says, "I want to do all the things that parents can't do. Even though it wasn't my decision to be childless, it can still be my decision to live a child-free life."

She rolls up her sleeve and shows me a beautiful tattoo covering her right bicep. It shows two sides of the head of a raven-haired, flapper-esque woman. One half has a subtle smile, the other a slight frown. Each half is partly concealed by ten diamonds. Courtney says the ten diamonds represent the ten embryos she had transferred. Beneath the two women are tattooed the words "Grief and Gratitude." This is Courtney's mantra.

"Grief and gratitude can coexist. Just because we have a happy life without children, doesn't mean we didn't want them."

* * *

Any regrets?

"No. We knew in our heart of hearts that it wasn't going to happen. My entire identity was sunk into being a parent, and quitting gave me a chance to stop that. It gave me a chance to re-explore who I am, who my husband is, who we are in a relationship, and how we are when we're not in crisis mode all the time. It's given us an opportunity to envision a life that we can actually have."

What if you hadn't quit?

"We'd be completely financially devastated. And we'd probably still have no real answers and still be waiting. Let's say we raised the one hundred thousand dollars it takes for surrogacy, then what does that give our child? We wouldn't be able to travel with them. To us, parenting meant teaching our child about other cultures, and that's what we wanted for our kid. Instead, they would have had a family that was always in debt."

What is the story you tell yourself about this quitting experience?

"The question was asked and answered. We tried, we did it, and we learned."

What tradeoffs did you accept by quitting?

"We have to redesign our lives. But that's all positive. Our life was built to include a child that's missing. We could choose to live a life where there was a missing piece, or we could choose to live a decidedly child-free life. We're not compromising; this isn't a consolation prize. Grief is separate. This *is* the outcome of our fertility journey, and it's positive. Do I get sad seeing people holding babies? Sure, but that's not the life I get."

What does this quitting story say about you?

"Everyone wants to tell me that I was so brave, but it wasn't bravery. It was audacity."

What makes you most proud of your quitting story?

"We didn't compromise. Our relationship is stronger than ever. We are still going to have a happy, fulfilled life. It's just not the one that we planned. I'm really proud of getting out of that place of despair."

"I wasn't willing to put up with _____."

"I wasn't willing to put up with living for a child that wasn't there."

I Quit the American Dream

"I had a great life. I had a stable job. I was in a long-term relationship, and we were talking about marriage. I lived in a beautiful, warm place that lots of people pay loads of money to visit. I was ready to buy a house."

Emily was primed for all of the things the average American works a lifetime to achieve. And it made sense she found herself on the precipice of the American Dream. If she wanted a white picket fence, she could have it.

She was the kind of person who always had a five-year plan. When she was growing up on a farm in rural Illinois, the seventh of eight kids, her plan was short and direct: 1) leave the country farm life, 2) study science in college, and 3) immediately move to Florida to establish residency and then attend the University of Miami's stellar graduate marine biology program. You could set your clock to it; I bet Emily set several.

"I was always a self-proclaimed perfectionist," she says.

There is a lot said in culture about Florida, so I won't belabor the stereotypes here, even though I love a good "Florida Man" meme as much as the next overly privileged misanthrope. But one of my favorite descriptions of Florida is from comedian and podcast host Marc Maron, who often exasperatingly describes the state as the end of the road for so many people. You can almost hear him sadly shaking his head when he says it and feel the bewilderment.

Like a lot of young people, and people who move to Florida, things didn't quite turn out as planned for Emily.

She hated the state. She describes feeling an incredible "culture shock" that made her decide against staying there for six-plus years to do graduate school.

So, her original life plan abruptly stopped in her first year living in Florida. There would be no marine biology career. But Emily was destined for success. She was a hard worker, a planner, and, of course, a perfectionist. She pivoted easily and found a new path as one of the first employees at an aquaculture start-up.

The role started out great. It put her on a path that resulted in her staying in Florida for six and a half years anyway. It was also the first step toward what most of us are raised to want: The American Dream of a stable job, good money, and a house filled with all the things a house requires.

"I learned an immense amount about start-ups and business and how you can bring real value into the world, and how you can think very differently about very traditional problems," Emily says. "We were trying to impact the food chain and how things had always been done in the industry. It really sparked in me this sense of 'wow, I can have an impact and I can change things.' It was really inspiring."

Emily didn't regret her choice to not get a PhD at all.

After four years at the start-up, she started to feel less connected to the company and had fewer opportunities to create impact. This was a result of her being so good at her job.

"I had helped build the company, and then we scaled it. Then, we had partnerships. Then, I automated it, so it was running smoothly. The turning point was this realization that I no longer had control over the company's future. The job became more about maintaining rather than building. My main job was just to make sure nothing went wrong."

Unlike in the early days and years, the success of the company was no longer on Emily's shoulders. There was no more impact she should make. It was hard for her to just sit back and enjoy her handiwork.

I am childless by choice (or as I once drunkenly told my mom, "My vagina is for recreation only,") but I imagine this is what parents must feel like after they are done raising their kids.

"I knew that if I wanted to have more control over my career and actually create things rather than maintain the status quo, I'd have to quit," Emily says with conviction. The learning comes in the process, not in the accomplishments, you know?"

It's easy to think of perfectionists and five-year planners as mere resume-builders focused on the outputs rather than the journey. I appreciate that Emily gives them (okay fine, us) a more noble gloss by making us look and sound far less transactional about our desire for achievement than we usually come across.

But it wasn't necessarily easy. Emily waffled back and forth on the decision to quit for a year and a half before finally doing it.

With good reason, she wasn't debating just quitting a job. She was debating quitting her entire way of living: in the pursuit of The American Dream.

On paper—and I'm sure there was a literal pros and cons list on her desk somewhere—Emily had everything. She was on the cusp of living what many would call the "the dream."

But one woman's paradise might be another's purgatory.

"It was all deeply unfulfilling for me," he says, her voice lowering.

Emily realized that, while her life was checking all the boxes that society tells us matter, a perfect picture is just that—a picture.

"Over time, I realized that it was all just a picture in my head. It wasn't just 'oh gee, everything isn't perfect, and so it's terrible.' It was that things *were* perfect, and I was still unfulfilled. I realized that the voices there in my head telling me to check these boxes were other people's voices, not my own. This wasn't what I wanted out of life."

This realization that maybe her entire life was worth leaving behind was very foreign to Emily; even quitting her job was a big deal.

"I was raised with a farm mentality. It didn't matter if it was snowing or raining or you had a bad day, you had to go chop the wood. You just work hard no matter what. In my younger years, I definitely absorbed that quitting meant you weren't strong, that you weren't capable, that you didn't have the endurance or the grit to follow through on something."

We're always told that life is a marathon. Hearing the stigma around quitting phrased in such physical, athletic terms makes sense. Don't a lot of people vomit and shit themselves during marathons?

It's interesting that Emily's upbringing didn't cause her to equate quitting with failure, as is so common.

"It was more inwardly hurtful than that," she explains. "Failing was fine, everyone fails, learns lessons, and moves on. It felt like I wasn't gritty enough to hustle it out and keep going. The fact that I couldn't work hard enough to achieve or get something out of it, to follow it through to the end, or that like I didn't have the endurance, that was deeply, deeply unsettling to me. I had identified myself by my work ethic and by what I'm capable of doing."

Life was always presented to Emily in very linear terms.

"My parents, my dad especially, really valued education. It was, 'You work hard in primary school so you can then work hard in high school and get into a good college, and if you work hard in college, then you can do whatever you want.'"

Ah, the transitive property of hard work; do this and you'll get that. I'm no stranger to this linear lie. I still feel the sting of being promised this false bill of goods: that hard work always pays off. It took me graduating from New York University with a near 4.0 and not getting a job; graduating from an Ivy League graduate program and not getting a job; getting paid virtually nothing in the job I did eventually get; and then being sexually harassed in my third month to realize what a scam it all is. I wish every perfectionist, high-achieving high schooler was pulled aside and told: "Hard work doesn't always pay off. So, you may as well not waste your time doing the 'right' things and instead work hard on what you love. Life doesn't have to be a marathon, but it sure can be long. Getting stuck doing something that isn't working for you is what makes it feel short for many people."

Emily's first big quit—leaving her start up job—was the transition that caused her to stop seeing life and quitting things in life in such black and white terms.

"I've reframed quitting for myself to now think of it as opening possibilities, instead of shutting them down."

It also gave her the courage to make an even bigger transition. She quit her pursuit of living The American Dream.

"I was on the path for which I was raised: marriage, house, probably kids, a dog, yard, a pool, a nice neighborhood in the suburbs…" she says, listlessly. "It was this kind of Midwest mentality ingrained in me that this is just what you do, and this is what life is about. That's where you find happiness and fulfillment."

She remembers a moment one Fall when she was walking along the beach with her friend, having a casual conversation. They were sharing gripes about their daily lives, as friends do. Emily found herself questioning her happiness out loud.

"There was this thought that hit me: Why isn't what I have enough? Why am I feeling so discontent? Shouldn't I just be grateful for what I have? Why is this unsettledness in me where I was thinking 'Oh, if I can just do this, or get that, then I'll feel better'? Don't I have enough to be happy? *Shouldn't* I be happy?"

The word "should" is so strong in us whenever we feel like our lives are going haywire. It can often drive us to one of two extremes: adding more to our lives (ex: the midlife crisis sports car) or subtracting things from our lives (ex: going monk with our possessions). For Emily, it was a matter of what was missing.

"There was creativity and inspiration missing in my life. Even in my social circle. Maybe it was just part of the culture of Florida, but you have a lot of 'convenience' friends who are just always available. They didn't offer a lot of substance or meaningful connection beyond just always being around."

Emily was changing but it didn't feel to her like anyone around her was going to follow suit.

"I felt like I was in this rut, and if I didn't get out of it soon, then it'd get too deep for me to ever get out. It felt like everybody around me was just like 'Well, that's just what you do.' But I didn't want to keep doing the same thing forever and ever."

It was simple moments like deciding what to do after work. Once she had gotten her start up into maintenance mode, she began to have more and more weekends free.

"I'd ask my friends or my boyfriend what do you want to do, and it was always the same: going down to the neighborhood bar. It was like a bad version of *Cheers*."

As someone who, as a childhood TV junkie, cried herself to sleep the night the final episode of *Cheers* aired, I'm secretly so happy that someone younger than me knows *Cheers*!

Even going to the beach got old for her in a way that it didn't for her social group. Every day seemed to present moments that showed her this wasn't her community any longer.

The people she was around, including her boyfriend, were very much about the acquisition of stuff and the classic "Keeping up with the Joneses."

"Everyone wanted a pool, a bigger car, a house, and lots of stuff. A lot of conversations were about so-and-so down the street just bought such-and-such. That sort of thing just never concerned me in life. That's not what brings me happiness. If your definition of happiness is having one of those giant mansions on the beach, you're going to be discontent with your life up until that happens, and even after."

She tried involving her boyfriend in her goal of getting music back into her life; they both used to play guitar before meeting each other, but it had been years since either had played. His response was tepid, and he seemed happy to leave the "remember we said we would..." labor to Emily. It never happened.

"At the time, I didn't know exactly what I wanted, but I did know deep down that something was missing: real connection, creativity, trying to put something good out into the world instead of just clocking in and clocking out. Trying to find some happiness in the gaps between work wasn't going to be enough for me."

One of her older brothers was instrumental in helping her find her way out. He also worked in tech, but in San Francisco. He had often given Emily advice through the years, including during the year and a half she was summoning the courage to quit her start-up job.

"Hearing him talk about San Francisco and his life and how he felt so clearly that he was *supposed* to be there...it made me realize that I'd never felt that way before. He helped me understand that I could quit this life system that I had built, that I could live my life a different way."

Much like with her start-up job, extricating herself from her life system and all the trappings of the American Dream she'd obtained was not easy.

First, her relationship with her boyfriend. It slowly deteriorated in the couple of months after she quit her job, and she began asking for things to change: how they communicated, how they spent their time, how they thought about the future.

"I wanted these changes, but I didn't get a feeling that there was any want or desire to change things on the other end. We even had this conversation where he literally said he was quite happy with his rut."

Then, the home ownership aspirations she'd had got stalled. Emily got offered a remote job that would eventually allow her to move to California if she wanted. She didn't renew the lease on her apartment rental.

"I realized I was not going to buy the house I had been planning to buy."

She accepted the job and stayed in Florida for a few months, essentially to allow for her relationship to end and give her time to sell her things and make the move to California. As with many quitters, the first big quit opens the door to other quits and makes them easier.

"Quitting my job was the start of this," she reflects. "That led to all this other quitting because I really wanted to leave this life system I'd built for myself."

A big part of Emily's new life in California includes being less consumerist. There are no Joneses with whom she wishes to keep up.

"I'm not some rock star minimalist, but I do try to live a conscious life where I consider what I consume and what I leave behind. I left behind probably ninety percent of my belongings in Florida; I just really narrowed down what was important to me and what I knew was irreplaceable."

In the two years since she moved, she's made the conscious choice not to just buy and replace everything she left behind. She finds herself most often sharing her quitting story with new roommates when they notice how few items she's moving in with!

"A key concept to quitting is that you have to change the status quo. You have to make a choice to change. You have to find your own momentum to choose change over what is familiar, easy, and 'normal.'"

I can understand—maybe—why quitting is so hard for people. Change, upending the status quo, and knowingly choosing discomfort and uncertainty is hard, perhaps even irrational. Most of our life decisions are explicitly about reducing uncertainty and minimizing risk. For most, even if the status quo sucks, it's easy to think that change is worse. So why take the risk? But that's just it; we've been duped into thinking that staying still and suffering through the status quo is less risky or less comfortable than change. We rarely actually know that to be true. Who is to say that taking a risk (if it involves quitting or not) isn't *less* risky than staying where you are?

Emily took the risk and quit.

* * *

What if you hadn't quit?

"I think I would have felt very tied to a life of mediocrity. I'd have all of my life needs met and then some, but I'd feel very blasé about it. If I hadn't quit and I hadn't left when I did, I'd be living the dream, but it wouldn't be my dream."

What tradeoffs did you accept by quitting?

"I went through all the discomfort and uncertainty of changing and wrestling with what it meant to be 'a quitter.' I left behind the dream, but all of that was worth it for the opportunity to build the life that I wanted."

What does this quitting story say about you?

"My story says that I think, deep down, I was meant for bigger things."

What makes you most proud of your quitting story?

"What makes me most proud about quitting is that I grew along the way, not only as a person but to fulfill bigger things that I'm capable of in the world. I used to think that perseverance was the end all be all. Reframing how

I thought about quitting was one of the greatest things to come out of my story, normalizing that I can grow as a person and change my mind about these rigid things that were from my childhood."

"I wasn't willing to put up with _____."

"I wasn't willing to put up with the status quo."

QUITTING PEOPLE & RELATIONSHIPS

I Quit My Mom

Cassie was the judge at her own criminal trial. She was also her own defense attorney and all witnesses.

The trial took place in New York in 2019, at a solo comedy festival called SOLOCOM. The courtroom was the stage. The audience was the jury.

"The People v. Cassandra Meliora," was Cassie's autobiographical one-woman show.[6] The show description read: *Judgment Day comes for everyone... even attorneys. What would you do if suddenly accused of heinous crimes by those closest to you? High-powered attorney Cassandra Meliora must combat a shadowy network of attackers to defend herself to you, the jury. Is she guilty? Is anyone innocent? And what's the right sentence for what she's done?*

The reference to being accused "by those closest to you" is intentionally vague; this scripted trial was undoubtedly about

---

6   Cassandra Meliora, "The People v. Cassandra Meliora," performed live on November 21, 2019, The People's Improv Theater, Solocom 2019.

Cassie's mother, the "shadowy" attacker Cassie had to defend herself from.

We all process complex relationships with family members in different ways; some of us go to extreme lengths to gain their approval and love; some keep them at an arm's distance, understanding the emotional limitations of blood bonds; for others, like Cassie, shared blood is not enough to sustain a relationship.

After nearly three years of not speaking with her mother, Cassie created this show to help process the very complex relationship she used to have with her mother. She took the insecurity and doubt that we all have when we are contemplating cutting a loved one out of our lives and literally went through a mock judicial process to help examine her feelings of emotional betrayal through an audience. It was her way of unpacking and litigating (literally) if she was responsible for what happened between them. Before Cassie quit her mother, she was definitely not the quitting type.

"My knee jerk reaction was always 'No, you shouldn't quit,'" she says. "You should try harder, you should commit more, you should dig deeper and find a way to follow through." I find myself instinctively nodding along as she says this. Though Cassie is an environmental attorney, I feel like her friendly face and intense demeanor would have made her an amazing youth sports coach in another life. She knows exactly where this anti-quitting ethos came from and how it deeply influenced her personality.

"The world has supported the idea that nothing is beyond your control. It's sort of a perversion of personal responsibility. It means that if you fail, it's your fault and no one else's. And so, you should just try harder because you're the only one who can make it right."

When Cassie describes this very common "quitters never win" ethos, it starts to sound sort of messianic. If quitters never win, and we are the only ones responsible for choosing to quit or not, then the world is a very lonely place indeed.

Her upbringing and family also contributed to this worldview.

"In my family, success was just assumed," she says. "*Of course*, you'll get all A's, *of course*, you'll get this prestigious scholarship, *of course*, you'll succeed in all these things. And so, there wasn't really any joy in succeeding because it was just the baseline, the bare minimum."

This instantly makes me think of something that I believe is unique to my South Asian culture: parents aren't supposed to complement their children because it's supposed to be bad luck; it will draw the "evil eye" toward the child. There is even a quickie prayer a parent is supposed to say to ward off bad luck whenever someone *else* pays their child a complement. I appreciate some of what this created in me: independence, not relying on the approval or validation of others, etc... but, Jesus Christ, sometimes it'd be nice to hear your parents say you look nice in that dress, or you totally deserved to be elected class president...or even just a "you're a good person." To be complimented was to be cursed. The "Are you praising your children too much?" genre of commentary that seems to be common in recent years makes me chuckle.

But while success was expected and Cassie and her four siblings didn't get too much credit for their achievements, failures were another matter.

"There was this sense that the only way bad things happen is if someone is robbing you of it, or there's some conspiracy or something horrible," she explains. "If you have total control, why would you allow that to happen? It makes you feel that if something isn't working, it's because of you. It definitely led me to overestimate just how much I can control and how much I can muscle my way through things."

In this worldview, you get no credit for your successes but all the blame for your failures. There is no path to be admired, respected, or even complimented.

As you might imagine, quitting was not an option for Cassie growing up. She recalls one of the rare occasions she wanted to quit an activity. She was in eighth grade and it was time for National History Day, a multi-category competition for which Cassie chose to research a historical figure and do an individual performance of them. Cassie's school program was very small; she was one of only a handful of students that went to the national competition in Maryland, with one teacher as chaperone.

"This chaperone got really mad at me because he couldn't find me. I was just calling my mom [from the payphone] at the time, but instead of saying he was scared by not knowing where I was, he viciously laid into me. And so, I didn't want to do the program anymore if it meant I was going to have to be around this person."

Not only did Cassie's mom not let her quit in that moment, but Cassie also continued doing the program for years afterward. To quit was to fail, and that was not allowed.

"It's hard to know what my mom really thinks," she says, "but I assume it's a combination of both of my parents being the first in their families to go to college. For them, educational excellence and extracurriculars are super important. That is how you 'make it.'"

For all the "model minority" and "Tiger Mom" nonsense that exists for Asian-Americans like me, it's gratifying to hear that this pressure-filled dynamic exists in white American families, too. It's no secret that many immigrant parents view their children as extensions of themselves. Cassie's South Dakotan, white mother was no different.

"I don't think she's able to see a distinction between herself and her children," Cassie says. "So, if she couldn't understand or feel what we were feeling, or comprehend why we wanted to quit something, it didn't matter to her. We weren't allowed to have our own feelings. I got really used to the idea that how I felt about something, whether or not I enjoyed something, was not relevant information."

For some, this "personal responsibility" / "it's all up to me" kind of narrative all too easily slides into narcissism and messianism. It's the toxic underbelly of the myth of American "individualism."

For Cassie, though, this narrative led to self-doubt, anxiety, and stress. Despite doing all of the things her mother insisted upon: becoming a lawyer, "making it" in cities like Washington, DC, and Seattle, she lacked confidence in understanding what she wanted in life and what she didn't. Deciding to leave Seattle and return to Washington DC shortly before she and I spoke was a moment when Cassie was confronted with this dilemma.

"It was like, 'Why can't I make Seattle work?'" she faux wails. "'What is wrong with me? I'm supposed to be for everyone, every place, every job... I can do anything. Why can't I do this?'"

This brings to mind a quote from a well-known actor I read years ago. He said something to the effect of how being a high-achieving kid and getting into Harvard prepared him for being an actor; he insinuated that, at a young age, he got used to being everything to everyone, playing whatever role they needed him to play.

It makes sense that Cassie used the stage to validate that she could not be everything to everyone... especially not to her mother.

The truth was Cassie just wasn't happy in Seattle. That was it. Simple. But she was so used to having her feelings denied that she didn't even recognize them when she had them.

Even passing, casual comments would elicit her mother's "never quit" attitude.

"I remember taking my first law firm job at a time when the [federal] government was shut down and there weren't a lot of options. I took it knowing that it wouldn't really be a forever job. I was chatting with my mom one day and casually expressed thinking about what I'd do after this job, and she cut me off and just said, 'No, stay in this job forever. Make a ton of money. And that's it. I don't want to hear anything else.'"

There was not a lot of room for error; let alone exploration or pivoting. Nor room for Cassie to figure out what she wanted in life, especially if that included quitting something.

It's amazing that Cassie, with the "quitting is bad" mindset she was raised with, did ultimately quit the source of this mindset: her mother. Her four siblings ultimately did too, most of them before Cassie did. But because Cassie spent many years being the glue that held her family together, that decision to quit her mom was delayed.

"I took on a pretty big role in feeling responsible for keeping the family together, kind of being the mini go-between marriage counselor for my parents, the one reaching out to suggest ideas for family trips, etc..."

I can sense how Cassie tried so hard to will her family into being what she needed it to be. I now feel weird and sad, instead of joyful and entertained, about the lengths the two little girls in *The Parent Trap* went to.

Of course, having a mother who demands high achievement from her children not only frames Cassie's outlook on quitting but also sets up the difficulty for her to ultimately sever the relationship.

She compares her mother to Adnan's cousin in the true-crime podcast, *Serial.*

"If I was charged with murder, my mom would be the one going into the police department demanding records, sitting in a dank basement for hours and hours, holding a single sign protesting outside the governor's office. I had a mother, who for all her faults, would go to the ends of the earth for me. I had this impression of her as someone who was so loyal and so committed to her kids."

Cassie had this impression for good reason.

In her freshman year of college, she wanted to take more than the expected number of credits. The administration wouldn't allow her to, and there was a lot of back and forth. Eventually, her mother drove Cassie over to the office of the head of the honors program, and she argued with him until he relented.

"It was embarrassing, but she got shit done," Cassie says admiringly. "She went to the mat and raised hell for us in a lot of ways."

As Cassie got older, though, she began to realize that this fierce loyalty was not unconditional. It became crystal clear to her that her mother's fealty had contingencies during a family trip to Disney World.

Depending on your personal experience, you may be surprised that a family came totally, irreparably undone during a visit to the Happiest Place on Earth™...or you may not.

This was one of the travel plans Cassie had spearheaded for her family; after much discussion and back and forth, she gave up on an international trip and busied herself with planning a trip of compromise to Orlando, Florida. She secretly hoped this would be the baby step her family needed to eventually go out of the country together.

"This was a big occasion," she points out. "Me and one of my sisters flew. My mom and dad and my younger siblings drove from South Dakota."

The wheels came off the moment her mom showed up at the house they had rented for the trip. Cassie was twenty-eight years old at the time. She'd been a lawyer for three years. She hadn't been home to South Dakota in almost ten years. She was anticipating a joyful reunion with her family, an initial meet and greet filled with "How was your trip?" and "What should we do first?"

Instead, Cassie was immediately presented with an opportunity to prove her loyalty to her mother.

"'She comes into the house and, right off the bat, she starts complaining to me about how terrible my dad was on the drive and he said this, and he said that...Growing up, I was definitely the one she'd complain to about my dad all the time. Sometimes, I'd try to intercede and get them to understand each other, sometimes even outright telling him off and that he should be less mean to her. All of these things were definitely not my job," she acknowledges, "but I took them on."

Cassie wasn't willing to play the role of her mom's loyal confidante in that moment.

"I just said, 'Yeah, that sounds shitty, you should talk to him about it.' I will not forget the look of betrayal on her face. It was like I had slapped her."

This was a supreme act of non-compliance in Cassie's family.

"You never knew in my household what issue or stressor you did might set my mom off or set my dad off," she says. "And then there's this big, horrible chain reaction. You always felt responsible, partly because my mom would tell us directly, we were responsible. Nothing could ever be wrong due to people not being responsible for themselves. We kids felt like we couldn't mess up because that would trigger big responses in our parents, and everything would go to hell in a handbasket really quickly. The amount of walking on eggshells we had to do, it was kind of like living with alcoholics except nobody drank."

The family photos document how Cassie coped in her own way as a child. From about age eight to fourteen, Cassie would always appear grumpy or crying in the family photos taken at gatherings and vacations.

"I realize now that those were the few moments where they needed something from me that I could withhold. They needed me to be there and to actually look happy and smile for the camera. As stupid as it sounds, it was one of the few times that I could assert that I mattered."

During the rest of the Disney World trip. Cassie's mom repeatedly brought up what had happened between them, once claiming that Cassie had laughed in her face and advised her to talk to her "abuser." Cassie received the cold shoulder from her mom the entire time. She got through the vacation with a "combination of ignoring it and placating it."

The vacation ended, but her mom's sense of betrayal did not. For the next two and a half months, Cassie and her older sisters, even the one who didn't go on the vacation, would receive dozens of text messages every day from their mom about that incident as well as a post-vacation argument their mom had had with one of Cassie's older sisters.

The texts were "a combination of mean-spirited things and things that didn't make sense," Cassie remembers. "One month after they began, I woke up and saw that she had texted me at 3:30 a.m. her time, that she doesn't think she has a family, she just has a portrait of a family."

This brought Cassie to tears.

"I was really proud of how close I thought we were. I really loved my mom. The way I thought my mom loved me was the foundation for my sense of safety and how I understood my value in the world."

Cassie couldn't understand how she and her mom had gotten to this point, a couple of months after what should have been a minor tiff at Disney World but had snowballed into weeks and weeks of constant harassment.

"This very minute thing just unleashed this torrent of horrible stuff from my mom. I just felt crazy." She calls herself "crazy" rather than placing responsibility for the situation on her mom. It makes sense; she was raised to view failures as hers and hers alone.

Through the tears, Cassie found a silver lining.

"My mom finally did something that was too big for us to ignore."

In her one-woman show, Cassie references an email her dad had sent her during all of this in which he described her mom as being "on the warpath" and expressed his doubts on what would stop her behavior absent a mental health commitment or the police. This scared Cassie, especially since her dad was not prone to exaggeration.

Quitting things is hard for most mortals. Quitting family relationships can sometimes take Herculean emotional strength. It took Cassie a year and a half to get there.

That year and a half contained all the expected up and downs, uncertainties, and eggshell-walking-from-a-distance you might imagine.

"I would try to engage and re-engage her. I'd try to offer her advice on handling a falling out with someone else. I offered to go to therapy with her to talk things out. One time I wrote her this really long, heartfelt email about where I was coming from, and how I'm hurt, and asking to hear her side. All I got back was complete nonsense."

One of the many times Cassie's mom rejected the idea of therapy, her reason was that she had seen a psychiatrist many years earlier and he had said there was nothing wrong with her.

Cassie is justifiably incredulous. "No psychiatrist has ever said that!"

True to her upbringing, Cassie *tried* and *tried* and *tried* to fix the relationship with her mom. She thought she had control.

"Nothing I did worked. I'd try to set boundaries on when she should text me, and she'd ignore them. It became clear to me that she never cared about what I thought or how I felt about anything."

Cassie eventually blocked her mom's cell phone. It's been five years since she's spoken to her, and there has been very limited non-verbal contact. Her dad calls her only when he is not in physical proximity to her mother; the risk of her grabbing the phone and speaking to Cassie against her wishes is too high.

The longest I've ever gone without speaking to my parents was two months. We got into an argument after they found an essay I'd written in a college social criticism class that was published online. It was 2005, and they are parents, so I have no clue how they navigated their stone tablets to Ask

Jeeves to even find my essay, but they did. And they were not happy with what I had to say about anti-Blackness and colorism in South Asian culture. They asked me to take the essay down; I refused.

South Asians love to emphasize that family is the most important thing; but in my experience, it's often just a means to take your family for granted and treat them hurtfully with no consequences. Every family says hurtful things to each other, for sure. But apologies are rare in my experience. Arguments like the one I had with them over the article never have any conclusion or resolution. We just adopt a "we're family so get over it"/ "What are you going to do about it?" mentality.

I don't know why family has the ability to bring out the worst in us...or is it that we reserve the worst of ourselves for our families? I've seen my mom react calmly and neutrally when faced with racism against her; I'm a thousand percent certain she's never called anyone a "liar" to their face... except me, when she wanted to dispute the memories and thoughts I expressed in that essay. The only people who have ever called me a bitch to my face are members of my family.

If we treated our friends the way we treat our family, we'd have exactly zero friends. Just because you are family doesn't mean you can get away with not treating each other like human beings. I only quit them for two months before I unwittingly caved and let things go back to their dysfunctional normal. I'm incredibly impressed Cassie has made it five years.

"I still don't think she has any understanding of why what she did was wrong," Cassie says of her mother. "In her mind, it's one of two extremes: either I'm a terrible daughter or I've been manipulated by my sisters, or everything is fine we don't have to talk about anything. But either way, she gets to decide. There's never a middle ground. Either way, nothing I do or feel matters."

The little email contact Cassie has had with her mom since she decided to quit her has been toxic and dramatic.

"She sent an email to us one year that referenced a woman who had killed herself. She included this woman's suicide note in the email, mentioning that the phrase "sadness sinks in deep" resonated with her, and who else in the family might be feeling this way? Oh, 'and you all should come home for Thanksgiving.'"

Cassie is still in awe of the tone deafness her mom demonstrated in the email.

"What a horrible thing to send me, you know? Not only is it horrible to me, but there is a real person who is dead. What planet do you live on where you think this email would encourage me to ever spend time with you again? She can't even see how things like this are driving an even deeper wedge between us."

Cassie felt vindicated in her decision to give up on her relationship with her mother.

"This is a person who just cannot be reached. I'm powerless."

If with great power comes great responsibility, then it might be reasonable to expect that with the relinquishing of power can come great relief.

Cassie definitely felt unburdened.

"It was in some ways defeating, but in many ways very liberating. As much as I wish the way my mother had treated me had anything to do with it—and so then I could control it—the gift is that there is nothing I can do. I don't need to be a martyr. I don't need to give up my life to protect this illusion."

Cassie has sometimes wondered if she could ever un-quit her mother.

"I'm at a point where I don't think therapy would even work for us because I think she honestly doesn't believe there is anything wrong with her. So, I'm left with two options: either I carry on as I am and cut her out of my life, or I accept her as she is without her ever changing. I think that would require a level of peace and grace of which I don't think I'm capable." Five years into her quitting story, Cassie has a more finely honed understanding of her belief systems.

"It was really like experiencing the death of a dream I had. Death of all these illusions about my family and the death of my identity. I'm a really different person now, even if it's not in ways that people can necessarily see. It was a really strong core belief of mine that you don't quit on family. It doesn't matter what they need; you go to the ends of the earth. That's what family is. Realizing that I had limits on that belief and that I won't destroy myself for anyone, not even family...I wouldn't have understood that about myself before this."

Cassie has some regrets, but they aren't about her mother.

"If I could go back, I would try to handle myself better. I was so raw and radioactive, especially the first year, that I hurt a lot of people in my life. I regret hurting those people who had nothing to do with it."

But Cassie shows her newfound capacity to forgive herself almost instantly. She can't imagine how she would have or could have handled it differently. The only "practical" regret Cassie has is she wished she had mailed herself her baby photos.

"I will be cut off from a really big part of my roots, no matter what. Not having those photos is a physical representation of that loss."

While Cassie had early validation from some people that what was going on with her mother was strange and not appropriate, she was still confronted with "Oh, well, you can't just give up on your mom."

"I think society, in general, understands "bad dads" more than it does "bad moms,'" she reasons. "We have this culture of the 'deadbeat' dad, and there are movies about bad dads or the children of bad dads. There really aren't movies about women who cut off their moms because there aren't these societal models out there; it's hard for people to wrap their heads around what a mom could possibly do to have her daughter quit her."

Cassie, rightfully in my opinion, begrudges those along the way who have casually dismissed her choice or, worse, think her choice was made casually.

"My mom was so essential to my being and to my understanding of myself, my value, and what I thought love was. When people give me advice on what I should do to fix it or question whether it was really necessary for me to estrange myself from her, I get so mad and want to say: 'Do you really think I didn't try fucking hard enough? Do you really think I'd amputate my leg for fun?' The only thing I *didn't* do was give up on myself; that was the last choice I had left, to be subsumed by her, to stop being a separate person. I had to quit the person I was in order to live."

I've always felt this is one of the worst parts of anti-quitting culture: when others ambivalently lapse into victim-blaming by inquiring about what you did or didn't do, or offering unsolicited advice about what you should have or could have done. It's these sorts of reactions I'm sure Cassie has in mind when she shares how she used to be afraid of "people saying I couldn't hack it, that I didn't try hard enough, or that I gave up." It's so rare that anyone just accepts the choice and finds meaning in it by saying, "Wow, it must have been really bad if you gave *that* up." Judge the circumstances based on the action, not the action based on the circumstances.

Cassie now has the confident humility that quitting can bring.

"Now I'm sure that eighty percent of the things I've done in my life, no one gave a shit about," she says laughing.

She's able to retain that confidence even as she knows that quitting her mom wasn't a one-and-done deal. She's gone through the difficult process of deciding to quit; every day from now on, she'll have to continue to make that choice.

"Most of the real quitting focuses on removing the toxic patterns and messages she gave me that I then internalized," she says. "Ceasing communication with my Mom was a necessary but insufficient step to really quitting her." For Cassie, the true quitting is the ongoing internal work she has done and continues to do. As she describes: "Scooping out my insides and purifying them with nutritious, new experiences, like an emotional dialysis machine that runs on compassion."

* * *

When do you share this story with others?

"I feel like if I treat it as a lighter thing it's better than treating it as this deep, dark secret. I can mention it and then go in-depth later on if necessary. It feels more liberating for me to wear it on my sleeve. I find that I'm meeting more and more people who also have experienced estrangement from their families, and it becomes this nice opportunity to give each other company. When I meet new people and the topic of family origins comes up, I can now say 'I don't have a mother' as easily as I can say 'I have blue eyes.'"

What does this quitting story say about you?

"I feel like the defining struggle of my life has been to believe that I have value and that I get to need and want things. This doesn't make me a bad or selfish person. It's taken me a really long time to see failures as valuable and then to actually feel the joy of success."

"I think quitting my mom has made me a more compassionate person. I'm less likely to think that people who find themselves in bad situations messed up or deserve it."

What makes you most proud of your quitting story?

"I'm willing to talk about it. One reason I did 'The People v. Cassandra Meliora' was just to get the story out of my body. Another reason was the hope that it tells someone else that they're not a freak, there is nothing wrong with them if they have to make this choice."

What tradeoffs did you accept by quitting?

"It's tragic. I gave up an illusion; reality is much harder. But it's also the most important thing I've ever done. It sounds corny, but I had to give up my past to get my future."

"I wasn't willing to put up with _____."

"I wasn't willing to put up with being erased."

I Quit My Best Friend of Ten Years

———

Trigger Warning: sexual assault

Geeta thinks quitting can be both good and bad. A fellow South Asian living in America, she understands and values living in the gray and straddling two worlds.

"Quitting is a hard truth dichotomy in life," she says. "It's a good thing to quit when it's about letting go of things that no longer serve you. When you've come to terms with figuring out what no longer serves you, whether it's because something is toxic or because something is no longer giving you good energy, it's a time to reflect and see if quitting altogether will put you on a path to something better."

It's very hard to dispute any of this. I do want to point out, however, that many people seem to be more comfortable with phrases like "letting things go" or "moving on" rather than the hard consonants of "quitting" or "giving up." That even a proud and successful quitter like Geeta adopts these euphemisms says a lot about how much stigma and shame surrounds the act of quitting.

"Other times, I think quitting can mean you are just giving up," she continues. "And maybe you should have stuck it out and shown more resilience to see the light at the end of the tunnel."

No doubt that it requires resilience to stick something out that you'd rather ditch. But what I've also learned in talking with people about their quitting stories is that the act of quitting not only requires resilience but also *creates* resilience.

"Quitting is a very confusing notion," Geeta says. "A lot of times, it's an inner dialogue. Quitting can be a good or bad thing, but it really has to be a personal journey you go on, yourself, and not something you have to listen to from others. No one else can decide that for you."

She thinks back through the things she has quit in her life and identifies a pattern.

"It felt so easy in some circumstances to walk away from, say, a job in the past when it was clear something didn't align with my values and wasn't in touch with what my values were. In those moments, I was confident in that part of myself, so quitting was easy.

"Other times it was very difficult, and it took a while to get to that decision in times when I wasn't always sure about myself; I was questioning my values and my purpose."

She locates her point of view on the "difficult" kind of quitting to her upbringing as an immigrant to the United States.

"There's a lot of guilt in quitting," she says, "because you've seen these past generations before you stick it out in really uncomfortable situations and never complain. Whether it's a marriage, or a job, or a family dynamic, there are so many situations where the mantra is 'It is what it is.'"

I'm very familiar with this peculiar brand of fatalism in South Asian culture. On one hand, I envy the freedom of mind and spirit it must give people to be able to just throw up their emotional hands and surrender to their reality. The American in me, however, is a fighter and always focused on making things better. If I had a mantra, it would probably be "This sucks. Let's fix it." I think I've been a regular quitter of things for most of my adult life precisely because I have very little patience for passivity or resignation to circumstances.

In addition to being a proud quitter, I am a lifelong TV junkie. One of my all-time favorite TV moments is when, at the end of Series 2 of the *The Office* (UK), the character of Tim, who has been smitten with his former co-worker and obvious soul mate, Dawn, for years, learns she is moving to the United States with her longtime fiancée, Lee.[7] In his mockumentary-style video interview, Tim has all the spirit of a beaten dog; he's missed his chance with Dawn, and now it's too late. In a series of micro-expressions, you can see Tim's resignation

---

7   *The Office (UK)* Series 2, episode 6, "Interview" directed by Ricky Gervais and Stephen Merchant, written by Ricky Gervais and Stephen Merchant, featuring Ricky Gervais, Martin Freeman, and Mackenzie Crook, aired November 4, 2002, on BBC.

to his life's choices: dropping out of college, living with his mom, stuck in a dead-end job he doesn't respect. You see all of this flash across his face as he cowardly yet forcefully says "You can't change circumstances." You can tell he is trying to convince himself and that he knows he has failed. He abruptly stands up, says "Excuse me," and leaves the interview room. You immediately know that *it is on*. Tim is going to tell Dawn how he feels. He is going to try to change the circumstances he just got done saying couldn't be changed. He doesn't care if it fails, he's going to try. I love this moment so much. I fancy myself a "circumstance-changer" because of how strongly I identified with this scene when I first watched it.

It's no doubt strange that the "This sucks. Fix it," can-do attitude is as American as the "stick it out" attitude. Both co-exist and yet, it's the latter we seem to default to more often.

Geeta sums up the South Asian version of "stick it out" this way: "It's this sense of 'always be grateful for what you have because you have it better than most.' That may be true but at the same time, it makes it harder to quit because you have this inherent baggage that makes it harder to make that decision."

American, Puritan, immigrant...it doesn't matter. We all seem to find our cultural way to stigmatize quitting.

One of the most important things Geeta quit in her life was also the hardest. She quit her best friend, Miriam.

Geeta's experience with this friend over the ten years of their relationship is something to which we can all probably relate.

It was very one-sided. Geeta gave more of her time and emotional labor than she received. The lack of reciprocity was especially easy to ignore for so long because Geeta felt sorry for Miriam.

"She had a very tough upbringing, or at least that's what she told me over the years. It felt like I needed to be in this relationship because I needed to take care of this person. Even though she was a capable adult, I felt like I was looking out for the child version of her. I was giving and giving and just not, in the end, receiving anything back."

They had met in graduate school when Geeta needed to find a place to live at the last minute. She responded to a Craigslist ad. Miriam was the potential roommate, along with one other person.

"I remember thinking Miriam was really interesting and fun. There were things about the living situation that weren't working, but it helped that there was another roommate in the mix that could help balance the energy out. Plus, we were all so busy with grad school that we were barely home."

They lived together in Los Angeles for six months before Miriam moved to San Francisco. That's when their friendship bloomed.

"Once we didn't live together, we started to develop a really strong bond based on the common values we had," Geeta says. "We both believed strongly in the idea of 'chosen' families and the value of hard work and supporting your family financially."

They also identified with each other, as is common, due to their shared life stage. They were both balancing school, job searches, and setting up personal finances for the first time, and they supported each other in entering this new phase of adulthood. They also helped each other navigate romantic relationships. Three years later, Geeta also moved to San Francisco. Miriam was the welcome wagon she needed.

"She was the first person to give me this cushion when I arrived. I remember getting off the bus in Union Square with two bags. I walked over to her house and crashed with her for two weeks until I found my own place. I had landed on a Sunday and was starting my new job the very next day, so I was grateful."

The gratitude would soon be muddied by Geeta noticing some new, red flags.

"I saw her jump from relationship to relationship. Even with friendships, it felt like she was never very committed. She was always sucking in her girlfriends into her romantic relationships because there was always drama in every single relationship she had. Some of these men she'd be complaining about, I just thought were the nicest people!"

Even Miriam's non-romantic relationships weren't immune to the fabrication of drama. These friendships came and went as Miriam pitted these people against each other.

"There just seemed to be a lot of bidding, like who could take her side the most, who would be the most involved in her romantic relationships."

I can't help but think of Nikki when I hear about Miriam. Nikki, Kim, Jenn, and I were a tight foursome from the start of freshman year of college. Nikki was a bit of a red flag from the start; definitely a party girl, a bit of a pathological liar, and a drama queen who made everything about her (including, somehow, September 11th). We all decided to live together in a four-person dorm our sophomore year. On registration day, though, we were forced to split up. Kim and Jenn had already been freshman year roommates, so Nikki and I were going to share a dorm together. I remember Kim and Jenn pulling me aside to reassure me that they'd be just down the hall to "help out." Their worry was obvious... and warranted.

Throughout the sophomore year, there were multiple interventions held by Kim and Jenn, all with the same message for Nikki: please stop the drama. I eventually stopped going to them. I let the friendship die. The bummer of it was that I also lost my friendship with Kim and Jenn; they still wanted to hang out with Nikki, "because she's fun to go out with." That wasn't enough to sustain a friendship for me. I didn't want to manage Nikki-created drama anymore.

Geeta's involvement in negotiating Miriam-created drama is what eventually helped her to pierce the veil and realize what was going on.

"She actually convinced me to move in with her [two years ago] because she'd just had a very quick and intense relationship end. She was crying, saying she didn't want to be alone and saying it would be a good idea if we lived together again." Geeta was eager to be a good friend and "take care" of Miriam after her breakup. Despite already having her own apartment lined up, she moved into Miriam's.

It took just one week for Geeta to start doubting Miriam's story.

"She'd said that she and her ex had been talking seriously about marriage, but in the first week of me moving in, there were a lot of guys coming over. It was obvious that some of them she'd been talking to before the breakup. Nothing added up."

This deception was very triggering for Geeta and brought up a painful memory of another friendship.

"I had a really close friend in college. She'd asked me to go to a party with her to be her 'back-up.' She ended up leaving me at the party to go hang out with some guys. Someone slipped a date rape drug into my drink. I got sexually assaulted that night. When I was at the hospital and the cops were called, she painted *me* as the "party girl." Which was absolutely not true; the drink I had that night was my very first drink ever. I was shamed by peers for years because of the rumor that she was spreading that I was a party girl and because I was sexually assaulted."

Despite that betrayal, Geeta stayed in that friendship for another seven years. Loyalty is rightfully a laudable trait, but to what end?

"I just never felt strong enough to end it. Even when for years afterward, she would cast that night as a "crazy party" story, even though for me, it was an extremely traumatic experience."

The emotions she was having about her friendship with Miriam were terribly familiar.

"I felt very much taken for granted and manipulated. I was again sucked into something that wasn't serving me well," she says.

Miriam's stories about the men she was dating also didn't add up

"Sometimes, she'd claim that the relationship had been abusive," Geeta says. "And I'd intervene and talk to the guy and pretty soon I'd learn there was zero abuse. But there was a lot of manipulation on her part that left them confused. I recall her complaining about this one guy who bought her things she'd claim she'd bought for herself. Once I was able to get to the other side of the stories, I started to realize that some of the things she'd been doing with them were also happening with me. For example, I'd learn that sometimes the cause of conflict with her boyfriends was they caught her lying and stealing from them and then she'd get mad at them. These are things you never want to believe are happening; until you hear it from other people, and then you start to become more aware. Turns out she was also stealing from me."

The issue of her stuff disappearing created a bit of a mindfuck for Geeta. Her first instinct was to doubt herself and to seriously question her brain function. How could it be possible that her best friend and roommate were stealing from her? She started to take photos of where she left things. Shoes, electronics, money...not everything would always be where the photos proved she'd left them.

"After a couple of months of this happening, I tried to have a conversation with her about it, more from the stance of 'Am I going crazy?' Miriam got defensive and started to flip the situation back on me. She suddenly started asking me things, like if I had used up all of her face wash without replacing it. It was petty, childish reverse-game playing."

When the truth has so many different versions of it, and you can't even trust which version your friend is telling you, that's when you have a Nikki on your hands.

The impact of the manipulation, constant self-doubt, and staying in the friendship was felt well outside of Geeta's friendship with Miriam.

"I was sticking it out even though I became incredibly unhappy. I began to gain weight. I was stressed out all the time. I couldn't function at work because my whole life was consumed by taking care of this friend and living in this toxic situation. I was getting lost."

The lack of sunlight in Miriam's apartment was also a negative factor.

"I'm a very 'lightful' person and her apartment was so dark, there was hardly any light in it." Geeta did make attempts to improve the situation and save the friendship, including setting healthy boundaries and talking about her concerns but to no avail.

"It was obvious that I wasn't being heard," she says.

It took nearly a year, but Geeta finally found what she calls "the courage to quit and find that joy and light again."

She started working with a life coach while she was living with Miriam. It turned out to be pivotal.

"It really gave me the courage to ultimately say 'You know what, I quit. I quit not only this living situation but also this friendship.' I cared and still care deeply for her, but it was no longer working for me because my boundaries were not being respected. Our friendship wasn't a two-way thing; it wasn't feeling good anymore."

I can hear how difficult the decision was for Geeta in her voice, even though it's been more than a year since she decided to move out.

"A couple of months before I moved out, I had a conversation with her and openly said I don't think I can be in this friendship any longer; it's toxic and unhealthy for me. Even though I love you and care for you deeply, I can't do it."

What happened next was infuriating: nothing.

"It was as if we'd never had that conversation," Geeta says, clearly still baffled. "She just went along as if everything was normal. So, I had the same conversation with her over and over again; but I think it was mostly me trying to convince myself that I quit."

Geeta, of course, sees both the "bad" and the "good" in her quitting experience.

"It was one of the hardest things I've ever had to do because she was one of my closest friends in this city, which can be lonely sometimes. It's also one of the healthiest things I've done for myself in a long time. It opened up opportunities for so many healthier relationships and friendships in my life.

She retains gratitude for what she did have with Miriam.

"Our friendship served its purpose; we had some good times and some not-so-good times. Life has to move on. Sometimes, friendships have to end."

The wall next to Geeta in her apartment is almost entirely windows. The sunlight streams in.

* * *

Any Regrets?

"I wish I hadn't moved in with her the second time. I knew in my gut it was the wrong choice. I wish I had been stronger and set healthy boundaries from the start. I don't regret quitting the friendship because I'm much happier now. It's time to move forward."

What if you hadn't quit?

"I would still be unhappy, and I wouldn't have opened my heart and had the space and energy to meet a lot of the amazing people I have in my life now. These are the people who are meant to be in my life and who align with me."

What is the story you tell yourself about this quitting experience?

"It's never too late to learn lessons."

"As hard as it is to quit something that feels familiar to you, it's the right thing to do, sometimes, for you to live a healthier, stronger, more fulfilling life."

What tradeoffs did you accept by quitting?

"I did lose a group of mutual friends. I'm okay with that, even if it's hard."

What does this quitting story say about you?

"I still struggle with quitting in my inner dialogue, but quitting has given me a sense of realizing my own resilience to keep moving forward. When you open up your heart by quitting things, it's actually a good thing. It's forcing me to work through a lot of things that still hold me back from quitting the situations and people that no longer serve me."

What makes you most proud of your quitting story?

"I'm proud that I was able to get away from focusing on what others might think or on what the repercussions for others might be. I can focus on myself and give myself compassion and love. That's what gave me the right level of courage and resilience to quit."

What values does this quitting story say you have?

"Compassion for myself and for others, integrity, and courage."

"I wasn't willing to put up with _____."

"I wasn't willing to put up with dishonesty, with less than what's deserved, disrespect, and emotional manipulation."

I Quit My Marriage

———

I feel pretty fortunate that my first "big" quit was a low-stakes one. Quitting my first foray into improv comedy while I was in college wasn't a big deal. No one's life was upended because of it. I wonder if my class instructor even noticed.

But for some, like Mona, the very first time they quit is a doozy. In her case, the first time she recollects quitting *any-thing* was when she ended her first marriage.

In her Asian culture, divorce carries a lot of stigma and shame. The view of divorce as "quitting" just adds fuel to the fire. (Mona's specific Asian heritage is generalized to protect her privacy).

"Divorce is just something you don't do," she says. "It's very taboo. When you get married, it's for life."

When I decided to divorce my husband, I can't say that I was rushing to tell my family, but the quickly approaching holiday travel that would need to be rearranged forced my hand. I told my parents hardly a week after I told my husband. My reason to procrastinate on it had been that I didn't want to go through the hassle of updating them on three years' worth of a bad marriage they hadn't known anything about up until that point. My preference for delaying this discussion hadn't had anything to do with shame; it was emotional laziness.

Mona? She didn't tell a soul in her family until she had filed the paperwork.

"I didn't want to get convinced out of it," she explains. "I decided to put my foot down and take charge of my life. It was an exhilarating moment for me, it was the first time I felt empowered to make a decision."

As it turned out, she didn't need to be worried. Her family was supportive.

"It was extremely liberating to learn that a lot of these fears I'd had were in my own head."

Their reaction was a surprise in no small part because Mona's ex-husband was the only person she'd brought home of whom they had approved.

"My parents thought he was perfect for me. It kind of led to us hurrying the marriage without asking the important questions and making sure there aren't any deal breakers."

Her ex was great "on paper." Not only was he also Asian, he was getting a PhD in physics while Mona was getting her Master's in biology. A year after they met in New York, they both found themselves living in Philadelphia where a spark developed unexpectedly.

"We were touring around Philadelphia together; it wasn't supposed to be a date. But then I asked him about his dissertation, and when he started talking about it, I was just hooked." She smiles remembering how attractive she found his intellect in that moment.

They saw each other more often, and things moved fairly quickly. They started going to the same Buddhist temple together and merging friend groups.

"The first year of dating was very nice. We were kind of stuck in a routine, but it was nice. It was stable and steady." I imagine their first year of dating was much like Mona's voice: appealing, calm, gentle.

After six months of dating, he said he wanted to introduce her to his parents in Asia. It made sense that he meets her parents first since they were closer, back in New York. They went there together a few months later, and their approval of him was swift, but Mona going to Asia to meet his parents posed a problem.

"My parents are very traditional in the sense that a woman is not supposed to meet the groom's family until there is some notice of engagement."

Her dad said she wasn't allowed to go to Asia to meet her then boyfriend's family unless he proposed. The conversation Mona and her boyfriend had on the way back to Philadelphia included what she now thinks of as the first warning sign she should have noticed about their relationship.

"I asked him, 'Do you know how we should address this? What should we do?'" Mona was looking for solutions, a compromise. "Instead, he just reiterated that there was no way he could propose to me before his parents met me."

It was a frustrating catch-22. He wanted her to meet his parents before proposing. She couldn't meet his parents unless they were engaged.

"The fact that it was very difficult for him to make a decision without his parents' green light was a huge red flag for me."

Mona wasn't ready for an engagement or for marriage, and she sensed he wasn't either, but the fact that he put the onus on this invented parental requirement instead of saying "I'm not ready," was different. It was inventing an excuse rather than acknowledging what he really wanted.

She saw this brilliant, accomplished man, who graduated from the top of his class at the best university in Asia...who couldn't make life decisions on his own.

"I was seriously considering ending the relationship on the car ride back to Philadelphia," she says. "We didn't talk for five hours on the way back."

But something Mona's mom had told her early in the relationship changed her mind.

"Even before my mom had met him, she came to me and said it seems like he's a nice person. I think she liked the idea of him because he was Asian and in academia. He had all the specs she liked, you know? She said, 'I really think this guy could be a good fit for you and I think you have a tendency to quit relationships.'"

Mona admits that in her previous relationships, she'd had no problem walking away at the earliest red flag. Her longest relationship at that point had lasted just one year.

"I guess others viewed it as an unwillingness on my part to work through the issues. My mom encouraged me to resist the urge to break up so quickly and, instead, give it some time and consideration first."

Her mom's advice came to her mind during the car ride. She fought the urge to break up with him and just drop him off at his place. Instead, she drove them back to her apartment.

"We talked about it, and he said he needed some time to think about it. The next weekend we went up to New York again, and he basically proposed to my dad, but he didn't propose to me!" This was not romantic or amusing.

Nevertheless, she accepted the proposal and they became engaged. Soon after, they went to Asia, and she met his family. It went smoothly, but she also observed things that only confirmed what she saw in him during that car ride from New York to Philadelphia.

"He was obviously the favored son because he was the first son. He had older sisters who still babied him and did everything for him. I started to put things together. I decided to go forward with the engagement because it felt too late to back away from it now."

This issue of his lack of independence from his family would repeat itself throughout the marriage. The engagement was also short, only one month long, but that was enough time for the doubt to plant itself even deeper in Mona.

"I felt a little empty. It was that feeling you get when you know deep down it's not the right thing, that feeling that gnaws at you and unsettles you in your stomach."

The night before the wedding, she went to the Buddhist temple where her family goes and pleaded with the monk to accept her into the sisterhood and begged her to shave her head. The monk thought she was just getting cold feet and literally pushed her out of the temple.

Mona laughs, "So *that* was probably another very strong sign, right?"

On the wedding day, she broke out into tears right before she walked down the aisle, delaying the ceremony by thirty minutes.

Red flags and warning signs aside, the first year of marriage was positive.

"That first year was memorable. It was great. It couldn't have been better. We had our own routine where we'd come home to be together, and we'd cook together, and we'd watch the Big Bang Theory."

Like in any relationship, there were things that annoyed Mona. She was frustrated that she was managing all of the administrative things for their lives like calling Verizon or the locksmith, while he only focused on his academic research. He'd tell her it was because his English wasn't very good.

"I was like 'Dude, you just completed a PhD and postdoc in the United States. Your English is good.'" But she was willing to be patient with him and continue being the problem-solver.

"I understood that math and academia was his world. He lived a very simple life, and there were probably a lot of things he had to learn from scratch."

In hindsight, Mona has another theory about why the first year was so good.

"I never really put forward what I wanted, right? He was always talking about his goals, of wanting to solve these equations, and of always wanting to move back to Asia. I wanted to be supportive of that."

Despite Mona asking him several times to do so, he never applied for his green card.

"Even though it would have made it easier for him to get academic jobs without a sponsorship, he dragged his feet. His plan was to always move back to Asia. He was supposed to move back after his postdoc. I was the unexpected part." She had reservations about working in Asia, herself.

"I knew I didn't want to work for any Asian company because I understand the corporate culture there, and it's very antagonistic toward women. It was going to be hard for me to find work there, but I was trying to think of ways to be supportive of him and keep the option of moving to Asia alive."

Pondering a move to Asia is what got Mona thinking seriously about starting her own business. It would give her the flexibility she didn't have in her government job and would also potentially protect her from the work culture.

They say the first year of marriage is the hardest. But for Mona, it was the second year when things started to unravel. He got a two-year contract job at a university in Oregon.

"He asked me to go with him, but I didn't want to quit my job at the time. His job was only for two years with no guarantee of extension... and he'd always wanted to move back to Asia."

Mona, instead, told him to stay in Oregon and feel it out, see if he wanted to be there long term or not. They began a long-distance marriage.

I have had two long-distance relationships before. One, in college, when my boyfriend and I only saw each other just once a month. It sucked. The second was with my ex-husband before we got married. We saw each other much more frequently. That, still, also sucked. Mona and her husband? They only saw each other just four times a year. I can't imagine how difficult that must have been.

There are definitely some good things about a long-distance relationship. I remember enjoying getting my body hair waxed less often and saving money because of that! Your friendships with your girlfriends remain as strong as ever. Visiting feels like a vacation; you don't have to get into all the nonsense around who does dishes better, or why haven't you unpacked that moving box in four years, or did you yet again come home from work with zero ideas or ingredients for dinner? The hard parts, though, especially when you are in your twenties and thirties, include loneliness, easy jealousy, resentment that you can't control where you live, and far too much time to *think*.

Mona started to gain clarity from this thinking once she and her husband started living across the country from each other. She woke up most mornings with anxiety.

"Up until that point," she says, "I'd always had this image of where I needed to be in life. This was not it. The relationship was good, and things were going smoothly, but we started talking about having kids, and I was like, 'Oh my goodness, how am I going to have time to devote to me? I haven't even made it to what I want yet.'" The idea of starting her own business became even more attractive.

"I was feeling unchallenged and in a place that didn't really satisfy my expectations. I've always had high expectations for myself, and I wanted to do bigger and better things. I didn't want my life to just stop here. I felt like that's where it was going."

She started to more seriously pursue entrepreneurship. She wanted her husband to be as excited about it as she was.

"When I first started bouncing off crazy business ideas with him, he was very supportive. He'd give me feedback. But it was always on the surface… I don't think he ever took it seriously. He didn't really believe I would leave my very stable government job to do this. It felt like he was just entertaining me."

After a certain point, Mona went to him and said she was nearly ready to quit her job and focus on her business full-time. She suggested that if they tightened their wallets a bit, they could survive on one income for a while.

He essentially broke down.

"I don't even remember everything he said, but he did say 'I'm opposed.' He said that. He didn't even try to sugarcoat it." The shock in her voice shows that she's still in disbelief that those were his words.

Mona felt betrayed. To her, she'd always been supportive of his work and his dreams.

"He could have found a job anywhere, but he wanted to stay in academia, so it was harder. I never wanted him to change that. A job is more than just a means of earning income. I respected that he had these lofty goals, it was admirable and quite sexy."

She realized then and there that he didn't appreciate how she had tried to be supportive of his ambitions.

"You can deduce that he naturally expected me to be that way, to be supportive of him. Even when he himself was not going to be supportive of my dreams."

Mona being a supportive wife was an assumed, bare minimum expectation, but she couldn't expect an equally supportive husband.

In subsequent conversations, they hit the same wall about her desire to be an entrepreneur.

"It really hurt me after a while to realize that he was so consumed with how *he* was feeling about this. It wasn't about him, it was supposed to be about me and my goals and what he can do to help me reach them. I never came up, though. It was always just about how he felt it would be really bad."

The marital dance between bare minimum expectations of each other and respect and gratitude is a hard one to perform. It's especially difficult when you think you are going above and beyond, but are taken for granted. It's also hard when someone just plain refuses to do the hard thing for you, like support you in your career ambitions.

Mona recalls this as the "first big hit" their marriage took.

The next big hit would occur on a trip to Asia they took to see his family. It was very hard for Mona to take the entire month off work, but she wanted him to spend more time with his family, so she made it happen.

"I can't share everything, but I can say it was a very difficult trip for me. There were so many times during that trip that I had to explain to him that *I'm* his family and he needs to put me first. Then, I'd get accused of coming between him and his family."

It's hard when the person who is meant to be your partner isn't on your side. It's a terrible feeling to realize that your spouse isn't really your biggest fan after all, and that they will choose their own comfort over your needs every time.

When they returned to Philadelphia from Asia, they came back to a domestic disaster: their house had flooded while they were gone, and the roof had partially collapsed.

"You know what he did? He flew back to Oregon, as planned, the next day. He just left me there to deal with everything!" She says this through tears of laughter, it still sounds so preposterous to her even years after this experience left her without a kitchen, eating ramen every day for six months. That laughter is also a result of the benefits of time. In the moment, she was the understanding wife.

"I was like, okay, it's hard for him to take time off. What option did he have but to go back?" It was only after her divorce that this anecdote began to stick out for her.

"My male friends would be like 'I actually never liked that guy,' and they'd say it was because of the flooding story." As much as quitting should be a personal choice based on your needs and values, it can always help to have a third person's perspective.

This was another moment when Mona realized she had given more to the relationship than she had expected in return. In fact, she didn't have any expectations. Mona is engaged again. Her fiancé recently told her that he knows she is an independent, strong woman.

"He said, 'Don't feel like you need to do everything yourself. It really breaks my heart when I see you and how you've lived. Sometimes, you can let me do the heavy lifting.' I really appreciated him saying that because it's very different from the kind of person I was married to."

The person she was married to didn't come back to Philadelphia again until nearly four months later for Thanksgiving break. Mona still had starting her own business on the brain.

"After dinner one evening, I brought it up again, and I told him that I really needed to express what my passions are and let him know where I was coming from. I explained to him that my entire life, I've had this vision and goal of where I'd like to be... but I wasn't there yet. I said I need to be challenged, that I'm just not a nine-to-five person, and that if we are going to take risks, we need to take them now while we're still young and can afford to fail and get right back up."

After her impassioned explanation, he looked at her in silence for a few seconds.

"And then he says, 'I'm not a risk taker. I'm a nine-to-five guy. What you are talking about scares me. I don't know why you want to leave your safe government job with amazing health insurance.'" Mona's heart sank.

"I just felt like 'Oh my gosh, why haven't I realized this sooner? This runs contrary to everything that I stand for and everything I believe in.' For me, my principle is that life is about risks and growing and stretching yourself to the limit and seeing how resilient you are."

Having ended a marriage myself, I know all too well how sometimes you can feel like Chazz Palminteri's detective character in *The Usual Suspects*.[8] You don't see what's right in front of you for so long, but then once you start piecing things together, you realize the person in front of you has been showing you who they are the entire time. A big disconnect between my ex and myself was around him not doing things that were important to me. It's tempting to say this arose only in our final, bad three years of a six-year marriage and fourteen-year relationship, but the first moment I recall that disconnect appearing was actually right after we got married. We had agreed to divide writing the thank-you notes for our wedding gifts fifty-fifty; equity in emotional and administrative labor was always important to me. I wrote my fifty percent in a flash. He dilly-dallied, procrastinated, then just didn't do it. I got upset after nearly a year of reminding and asking him, and he seemed to suddenly invent a reason for not doing what he said he'd do: writing thank you notes wasn't something he "valued." After a year of hearing him say he'd write the notes, this was news to me. It didn't matter that I told him it was something that *I* valued, that showing appreciation to others was important to *me*. He wasn't going to—and didn't—do his share of the cards. In our final years of

---

8   *The Usual Suspects*, directed by Brian Singer (Gramercy Pictures 1995).

marriage, that situation would repeat itself endlessly: him not doing what he said he would do, inventing retroactive excuses for it, and in general not doing things that he knew mattered to me.

I've learned a lot about how I view and value partnership from this experience. Partnership is not about doing things for someone else only when it matches your real or conveniently invented values; it's about doing things for someone else even when they are hard for you, simply because you prioritize that person's comfort over your own.

Mona realized that her husband was not going to provide her this kind of partnership; he wasn't going to overcome his discomfort with risk to help her craft the life she wanted. They canceled their plans to go up to New York to celebrate Thanksgiving with her family.

"From what I know now, my family suspected that something was off. When we didn't go up for Christmas that same year, that's when I think they definitely knew something was up."

Her husband did still go to Philadelphia for the Christmas break. Mona's birthday was right around then, too. She booked a show for them to go see, and they had a really nice dinner together. The night before her birthday, he treated her friends in honor of her birthday. She started to think she wanted to try to make it work after all.

She brought up her becoming an entrepreneur again. She explained it in terms of taking a measured, calculated risk. She said she needed him to help her. He shut her down again.

She didn't sleep that night. The next morning was her birthday. She woke up and rolled over.

"I have something to tell you," she said. "I think we should get divorced."

He was silent for a moment. Then he said, "Okay, what do we have to do?" The day after her birthday, they walked to the courthouse together to file the petition to divorce.

Although I'm not a sentimental person or someone who believes in numerology, I am a fan of when dates and experiences are comically juxtaposed. Due to circumstances beyond my control (or care), my own elopement occurred on Friday the 13th; it always cracked me up. Our reception was a month later, also on the 13th. In the end, it rained on all three of my wedding event dates (there was also a shindig in India) ... turns out rain is only good luck if it happens at *one* of your weddings. Just a few weeks ago, I met with my lawyer to execute my updated will, cutting my soon to be legally ex-husband out of it entirely. As I was signing and dating the first document, I realized that day was our seventh wedding anniversary. I let out a giggle when I realized this. No better day to celebrate my freedom, right?

I understand the wry laugh Mona has when she smiles and says, "I asked for a divorce on my birthday." While so many in society still view divorce as a failure to be mourned, and even more view quitting as a failure of character, Mona's "failures" actually got her closer to what she wanted and needed, including her current fiancé.

"At this point, I guess I have a better idea or understanding of what I'm looking for and what's going to work for me. I'm able to have those difficult questions up front. I know it's no longer about only romance for me, although that is important. Partnership, though, is the priority."

She spent the few years after her divorce enjoying single life and taking the time to heal and reflect on what she wanted.

"I learned that I need to treat myself well and set my expectations high. There's nothing wrong with that."

She's also realized the parallels between pressures not to quit a marriage and the pressure she felt to not quit her stable government job.

"In the past, I think a lot of women felt like they had to stay married because of what society would think. If you go back even further, like a hundred years, a lot of women didn't have the means to support themselves. So, they would need the cooperation of their family to leave a marriage, not to mention the social finger-pointing that would follow. So, there was obviously a lot of pressure on women to stay in a marriage even when they were unhappy. Much like that, I think there's still a lot of pressure placed on individuals to stay in a job despite how it makes them feel and how stifling it might be to their own personal and professional growth. I think the world we live in today holds the resources to quit if we engineer it properly. I think we have the tools to move forward and be independent. For me, that's the lesson: we shouldn't care too much about what society says."

Just a few months before I spoke with Mona, six years after her divorce, she quit her nine-to-five job and started her business. She calls this quit the "sequel" to her first one.

* * *

Any regrets?

"No. I feel like I've tried everything. I gave the relationship a lot of chances, and sometimes people don't change. Understanding this person from afar has helped me to validate my decision even more. Given his temperament and his values, there's no way I would have ever been happy in that relationship. If I were to do it again, I think I would really take my time to get to know the person and make sure that there aren't any deal breakers and really understand that marriage is for the long haul."

"One regret I did have at one point was when I had a dream where I was holding this six- or seven- year-old boy. It felt like he was my son. I don't have any children right now. I think that if I had stayed married to my ex, I would have children now. That's one thing I may have regretted because I've always wanted kids. It was so nice to hold that boy in my dream. It was a very bizarre feeling, as if this child was supposed to come to me, but it couldn't because of what I had decided. I felt like I broke my promise with my ex, in a way. Honestly, it wouldn't have been a good environment for child rearing, especially because I was losing myself and my purpose. It worked out for the best for everyone."

What tradeoffs did you accept by quitting?

"The benefits definitely outweigh the detriments. In hindsight, though, it caused my parents a lot of pain, especially my mom. I could easily decide to just move away and not be a part of their community in New York, but they couldn't do that. So, they had to wake up every morning to that gossip and that nonsense. I realized at my sister's wedding, five years after the divorce, that it was still kept secret from some people! At the same time, I think it's very good for my parents because it's helped them to develop a sense of empathy for divorcees. Up until that point, they were critical of divorced women and would kind of blame them for having made the wrong life decisions. Now, they are far more positive about divorce, and they view it as a wise and courageous choice that anyone can make. They now view it as a new beginning or a foundation for a new start."

What does this quitting story say about you?

"It shows my courage. It shows that I'm not willing to live by someone else's rules or expectations. I'm willing to focus on my happiness and live this life as my own, as I should. I don't think I would have been able to describe myself in this way before I made that decision. That decision was so instrumental in shifting my view of myself as a person. It's helped to beef up my self-esteem in a lot of ways. It definitely took a five or six-year period to get there, but that gave me the time to focus on my values and life goals. It was actually a pretty exciting period for me and one of growth."

What makes you most proud of your quitting story?

"After I made the decision, it felt like I had broken free from this mold that we call society, this mold that we call our family values. It really helped me to realize that I've been super focused on making my parents happy and proud of me, and I've always put myself and my needs second, or third, or fourth. This was the first time I made a decision for myself that would impact my life so tremendously without thinking about anyone else. That, in and of itself, was so empowering and transformative. I don't think I can ever go back to being incarcerated in that mold."

What values does this quitting story say you have?

"I'm willing to stay true to what I believe is right for myself."

"I realized the importance of achieving something for myself. It's not something I can give up easily because it comes at a cost."

"Whenever someone tells me they have decided to get divorced, I say 'Courage to you' or 'Congratulations on having made that important step. I'm pretty sure all of that happened after long and hard reflection and thought, and it's definitely not an easy decision to make.' Just the fact that you've made a decision is reason for celebration, I think."

"I wasn't willing to put up with _____."

"I wasn't willing to put up with living with someone who didn't share the same values as me."

I Quit My Engagement
One Month Before
the Wedding

———

"It's a very fine line between running away from something because you aren't comfortable with discomfort and deciding to stay with discomfort because you aren't comfortable with quitting."

Excuse me while I go find some thread to stitch this statement from Manasi on a decorative pillow so I can remember it forever. Manasi isn't new to quitting. A self-described "eighty percent person" who struggles with the attention to detail required to take something across the finish line, she doesn't suffer from the completionist tendencies many quit-phobes have. She's accustomed to, for example, changing her job every two or three years.

"I tend to like change," she says. "Change is exciting to me."

But even Manasi struggled with the big life decision to get married.

"I was engaged to be married when I was twenty-six and I was not happy about it. The whole wedding process was making me really upset. I was constantly in tears. I felt all this pressure. I couldn't eat, I couldn't sleep. I lost mobility in my neck. I was miserable."

I'm one of the least "woo-woo" women you'll ever meet. I'm a South Asian who hates yoga. I don't meditate. I don't journal. I don't have a religion. I often joke that I have no internal life. Even I, with my history of back and neck injuries, believe in the mind-body connection. I immediately know what Manasi means when she says she lost mobility in her neck; it was due to all the psychological stress her body was taking on.

Manasi's is a classic "it's not you, it's me" situation. She openly characterizes the man she was engaged to as "amazing."

"Somewhere, deep down inside, I knew I didn't want to get married. I didn't want to get married." She says it out loud a third time for emphasis: "I did not want to get married." It's almost like she's chanting to ward off a curse.

"But it took me a long time to come to that conclusion," she continues. "It was really only a month before the wedding when I felt like my back was against the wall, and I just couldn't do it. So, I called it off."

This wasn't some shotgun wedding; Manasi and her fiancé had been engaged for two years.

"It was an epic quitting struggle that entire time. Deep down, I knew it wasn't the right thing, but I felt that if I stuck it out things would be different. We had already invested so much money, so I thought 'I can't back out now.'"

Their courtship was a mix of modernity and old-school romance. They met on a dating site for people of South Asian descent, shaadi.com. "Shaadi" means "wedding" in Hindi, so it's expected that people are going on to the site to find their husband or wife, not just a fling.

They went on a couple of dates, and then it got old-school, black and white movie romantic.

"He was in the military and he was leaving to go do basic training for a few months right after we had a few dates. I remember thinking he was very handsome, smart, and funny. He was also getting an engineering PhD from an amazing school. My parents were going to love this!"

Despite how good he was on paper, Manasi thought it would be just a few dates then he'd be out of her mind for months. But he had other plans.

"He started writing to me from basic training, I'd get a letter a week. At first, I was weirded out by it, because I was thinking, 'This guy has known me for a grand total of ten hours, why is he writing to me?'"

But Manasi also understood how being away from home and perhaps being lonely might lead someone to want to maintain a connection, even if it's brand new. With the benefit of a few years of reflection, Manasi also realizes that, at that time, she and he both had this plan in their heads that they should be married by a certain age and that they should have kids by a certain age. They were both rapidly approaching those ages.

He came back from basic training, and they continued dating for a few months.

"It was like starting over again," she remembers. "He had a fun group of roommates; I had a great group of friends. We used to host parties together all the time. It was really fun."

And then he proposed.

The proposal was as classically romantic as the letters from basic training. He proposed while they were in a hot air balloon over the mountains in Vermont. The proposal wasn't the problem for Manasi. It was the timing of it all.

"We had talked about our timelines and if what we had might end in marriage. I had said that before getting engaged to anyone, I wanted them to meet my family, I wanted to meet his, I wanted to be dating for more than a year…" She had a preferred order for things.

None of these things had happened by the time Manasi was in that hot air balloon.

"It was hard because I didn't want to break up with him," she says, "but I also didn't want to marry him. I wasn't ready to make that commitment."

She said 'Yes.'

"I remember thinking to myself, 'If I say no, the guy operating the hot air balloon is going to be like "This is awkward." She laughs hard thinking about this scenario, recalling how she prioritized a stranger's feelings over her own when making such a huge life decision.

"The engagement started off a little rocky because I felt I wasn't ready for it." She readily admits that she lacked the emotional maturity to do what she should have done then.

"I would have had open lines of communication with my potential partner and admit I'm not ready to make this big commitment at this time, and it would have been okay. But I didn't know how to do that, then. I didn't even really know what I wanted. So, I said yes."

She allowed herself to be excited but then the wedding planning began.

"In Indian culture, the perspective is that your wedding isn't yours. It's your parents'," Manasi explains.

Her parents had an arranged marriage in India. As was the custom, most of the wedding plans were made by the bride's parents. When Manasi made attempts to convince her mom that the wedding was about choices she and her fiancé wanted to make, her mom replied, "Well, then I don't ever get one." This left Manasi torn between her vision for how she wanted to take this major life step and wanting her mom to experience her dream—and fulfill her sense of duty—of planning her daughter's wedding.

Wedding planning sucks. I, like Manasi, had a longer than average two-year engagement, but it was because both my fiancé and I had said "Not it!" immediately after the proposal when it came to planning. We knew it was going to be stressful. We chilled for a year, basking in the "being engaged" part of it all, which is the only part people care about. Once you are married, people don't give a shit. I highly recommend a long engagement for just this reason.

I was also never one of those girls who thought about their wedding or what it would be like; I didn't even have a boyfriend till I was twenty-one so hell, I thought I was *never* going to get married! Some of my friends had wedding boxes and scrapbooks they made when they were twelve to consult when they got engaged. I was starting from scratch. I had no ideas except that I wanted good food and booze and no religion or speeches. I remember when my mom asked me if I knew what my "wedding colors" were going to be, I wanted to slap her across the face. I was so angry at the world that this was something about which I had to have an opinion. I got divorced before I ever got around to printing out any wedding photos and I have no memory of what the colors of my wedding were. Everyone still remembers the lamb and the whisky fondly, so I think I did all right.

At no point, however, did my wedding feel like it wasn't "ours." Both sets of parents just stood back and let us do our thing. It made something that was already going to be dreadful (Seriously DJ? I can't play my favorite Radiohead songs all night at the reception because everyone will be bummed out?), way less dreadful. Manasi had this whole other layer of nonsense on top of the normal nonsense that is wedding planning.

"I feel like in Western traditions, the families are there to help you with the wedding and to support you. They are meant to keep you together during the process. Our families didn't realize how fragile the underlying relationship already was and that it was likely to break under the additional pressures that got added during the wedding planning process," Manasi says. "I think both of us were following our plans. What we had was acceptable, you know? We liked each other, we each checked off each other's boxes. The challenge was that neither one of us was emotionally mature enough nor had experienced struggle before. So, when the struggle became *us*, neither one of us knew how to react."

When troubles started during their engagement, Manasi recalls the two of them not being able to problem-solve collaboratively, or without blame.

"We didn't trust each other or feel like we could depend on each other."

She remembers a moment when she was in India, and she and her fiancé were talking on the phone about the wedding favors, just a couple of months from what would be their final wedding date.

"I wanted to, instead of wedding favors, give a donation to a charity in our guests' names. He went on a tirade about how doing that would be so narcissistic and how, in his family, 'we don't brag about our donations.' It was all so over the top. There were many little issues leading up to this one, but this moment really showed me that the trust we had with each other, the ability to give each other the benefit of the doubt, had eroded…or maybe never existed."

Luckily, Manasi had some people in her life to go to for advice. She spent the three weeks following the argument over wedding favors asking for help. She had an uncle who was only twelve years older than her. He and his wife had to battle family opposition to their relationship for many years. She asked her aunt and uncle what had made not giving up, persisting, worth it.

"They told me that they knew they were each other's people," Manasi says, smiling. "They were who they'd go to for everything. Even when their parents forced them to break up, they would still talk to each other about everything. It was very clear to them that they were going to be in each other's lives no matter what."

One of Manasi's friends also provided her with perspective and advice that she calls the best she ever got because it was so "non-romantic."

"She said the way she knew she wanted to marry her husband, even after years of resisting dating him, was that she just wanted him around. She wanted him around more than she didn't."

I love this non-romantic advice so much; I think it also should be stitched on a pillow! Humans tend to overcomplicate things, so I love it when someone like Manasi's friend uses human reasoning skills to distill love into something so simple. It is relationship advice that Manasi often gives to friends now.

Manasi also sought out a marriage counselor. She found a woman online who specializes in "sad brides to be."

"She's the one who told me that I need to be excited and happy about marrying the person you have *today*. Getting married turns today into that marriage. If you're not excited about that, then you shouldn't get married."

Family conflicts and arguments between Manasi and her fiancé added up to three wedding date postponements over the two years. During this time, Manasi obviously got to know her fiancé more than she did in their one year of dating.

A couple of key things dawned on her during this period.

"I realized that he had this image or vision of what he wanted for his life, and he was going to create it, no matter what. I was a good piece in the puzzle, but it wasn't about me. I felt like it could have been anyone who checked the same boxes for him. I was filling a role in his head."

Their different world views were also coming to light during this time. During wedding planning, Manasi changed jobs (again!), this time to a role that took her to Africa, Asia, and Europe frequently. Her perspective shifted to one that was quite different from her "pro-Texas, pro-America, pro-military" fiancé.

"I was understanding that there were really cool things about other countries that were bad about America and he couldn't deal with that. He couldn't deal with me criticizing this country."

Manasi believes that he also didn't want to get married to her.

"To be honest, I also had a plan and a vision, and he fit the image. I was in love with the idea of what we could be, but I wasn't in love with *him*, yet. That was my other realization during that time, was that we didn't become a team. We were still individual players. I was going to be marrying him for the potential, not for the 'what is.'"

It was her keen eye for change that helped her know this.

"Everyone will change, people will change, relationships will change no matter what. So, you better be really happy with the current state of everything."

Having been through a marriage that ended, I can attest that yes, people and relationships change. You hope your partnership will change for the better over time, not for the worse. In the absence of a crystal ball, the only information you can go on is what is right in front of you, what your partner has proven to be at the time you decide to commit to them.

Manasi is clearly a thoughtful person who was taking stock of her engagement from day one. Why did it take two years to call it off?

"It's a big deal to call off an engagement, right?" she says. "There was a lot of shame involved, a lot of disappointing other people, and disappointing myself. I worried, 'What if this is the best I can get? What if I never find anybody else?' I had struggled with dating and hadn't had any serious relationships since college. I kept telling myself that no relationship is perfect."

This is the danger of quitting and also of *not* quitting: you can't predict the future. We let ourselves believe that "sticking it out" is somehow less risky. So, sometimes we get stuck forcing ourselves to accept less than we want or what we deserve because we diminish ourselves into thinking this is the best we can do.

After three weeks of advice-gathering following the wedding favor incident, Manasi went to her fiancé and told him that she wasn't ready to make the commitment and that she wanted to postpone the wedding indefinitely and continue to work on their relationship.

He said no.

"He said we'd postponed it enough. 'Either you're ready or you're not. I don't want to keep waiting for you to make a decision. Tell me tomorrow.'"

She went home and thought about it. The next day, she went to his condo and gave him the ring back and left.

"Then, I called his parents and told them what had happened, that they might want to come to town because I'm pretty sure he's sad."

Manasi rallied some friends and found a truck and got all her stuff out of his place. Within a couple of hours, their lives were separate.

"I knew I did the right thing," she says, "because everyone around me told me that once the relationship was over, I was happier. The words they used were 'It was like your light came back.'"

It turns out Manasi was spot-on in feeling like she was just checking a box, filling a destiny that was only his:

"A few years later, my parents showed me this newspaper announcement about him marrying another girl. It was the exact same story that I had with him. He met her right before he was going to deploy, they wrote letters back and forth to each other, and they were engaged within six months of him getting back. He had a story he wanted, and he made it happen. He was going to keep trying until he got it."

He wasn't willing to change—or quit—it seems. But Manasi was willing to do so, and that made all the difference.

* * *

Any regrets?

"If I could do it over again, I would have recognized that I didn't want to get married to him in the first place and not put everybody through a prolonged, two-year process. I could have saved a lot of people a lot of heartache, including myself, if I had just been open about my feelings. It's hard to be tough on yourself when you're not emotionally experienced, and hindsight is always twenty-twenty."

"It was such a transformative experience for me that I would never take it back. This whole situation became very defining for me. I grew up a lot in the process. I made my own decision; I became an adult. It was from that moment onwards that I stopped letting expectations influence my life and tried to lean into what I want, what I need, and what I feel."

What if you hadn't quit?

"I don't know… maybe I'd be married to him with five children and not even aware enough to notice that I'm unhappy. Or maybe we'd be divorced. Maybe I wouldn't be who I am now, which is a person who is so into change, excitement, and being a trailblazer because I wouldn't have had that 'everything falls apart' experience. I think I'd be a really different person, but I might still be happy."

What is the story you tell yourself about this quitting experience?

"I tried my best. I tried as hard as I possibly could for as long as I possibly could. It wasn't the right thing, and I had to act on that."

"I had what life was supposed to be like. I didn't want it. I actively ended it. So, now there was no more template to follow, and it really let me be free to experience life as it came to me and live in the moment. It changed everything because I realized I wasn't living my life off a template anymore."

What tradeoffs did you accept by quitting?

"I traded the dream and the plan I had for my life for freedom to operate. It's ten years later, and I still don't have that dream of marriage and kids, but I've had an amazing past ten years, and I can't imagine doing it any differently."

What does this quitting story say about you?

"I think it says that I'm not afraid to make a really hard or unpopular decision if it's the right thing to do."

"I'm willing to inconvenience a ton of people!"

"At the end of the day, I'm going to put myself first."

What makes you most proud of your quitting story?

"I called his parents. It was a really hard thing to do. We didn't have a great relationship, and I didn't have to do it, but I wanted them to hear it from me and not blame him or wonder. I didn't want him to have to tell them."

"Now, I say yes to things more... even the smallest things. It's changed my day-to-day attitude, to say 'yes' to something even if I don't know what the end looks like."

What values does this quitting story say you have?

"I should have done it sooner, but, at the end of the day, there was authenticity and integrity there. I tried to do right by everybody as much as I could. I tried to do right by myself and be who I am. I didn't want to be constrained by something that wasn't a good decision for me."

"I wasn't willing to put up with _____."

"I wasn't willing to put up with feeling like he stole my light."

I QUIT THIS BOOK

Coonoor spent nine months writing a book titled, *I Quit! The Life-Affirming Joy of Giving Up*, the idea for which she had for many years before actually sitting down to write it. She eventually decided to quit writing the book because the book was done, disappointing her delightfully smartass friends who said she'd be a hypocrite if she actually finished it.

Any regrets?

"None! Especially since I had the idea for so many years before I actually wrote it. I only quit the book because I felt it was complete, or at least as complete as time and my publisher's patience allowed. I would have loved to include each of the nearly forty stories that people have shared with me, but the process of "killing your babies" was a positive one. I can't get everything I want. Perhaps there will be a second book where I can include those other amazing stories. I reserve the right to un-quit this quit!"

What if you hadn't quit?

"You wouldn't be reading this right now. There would be no book. My editor and publisher would hate me. But worst of all, I'd still have this idea gnawing at my brain just waiting to get out. I'd have regret over not getting my thoughts out there."

What is the story you tell yourself about this quitting experience?

"It was great! Five out of five stars! I can now get back to my non-author life, which I hope includes more time to exercise and less eating like an unsupervised twelve-year-old boy."

What tradeoffs did you accept by quitting?

"I no longer have a built-in excuse to say 'no' to things. 'I have to work on my book' is an incredibly powerful get-out-of-jail-free card. I'll now have to find other ways to spend my evenings that don't include the couch and a glass of wine."

What does this quitting story say about you?

"I've gotten over my perfectionist tendencies. I love the phrase 'Perfect means never.' If I had waited until I thought this book was perfect, it would never have existed."

What makes you most proud of your quitting story?

"To quit writing this book means I actually wrote a freakin' book! I did a thing, and now I have tangible, hold-it-in-your-hands proof that I did it. This book also allowed me to have incredible conversations with some amazing people, all of whom deepened my own understanding of why I am so pro-quitting."

What values does this quitting story say you have?

"Vulnerability. Authenticity. Taking risks. Questioning the status quo. Sharing myself with others."

"I wasn't willing to put up with _____."

"I wasn't willing to put up with letting an idea live the unfulfilled life of remaining just an idea."

Additional Resources

———

For more information and resources, including the *I Quit! Toolkit*, visit www.iquitbook.com

Acknowledgements

_____

If you got here, that means you didn't quit this book! Or perhaps you decided to quit it mid-way through and it happened to fall open to this page after you flung it against the wall, and it fell to the floor. Either way, welcome! I'm grateful regardless of the path you took to get here because it's an important one. Here I get to re-do my horrible, just *horrible* thank you speech after being crowned homecoming queen in high school and adequately express my thanks to those without whom I could not have done this.

Kusum Auntie, the first thing you said when I told you I was writing a book was "Let me be an early reader for you!" Your support during this process, start to finish, has been extraordinary. You helped me retain my excitement even in moments when I wasn't enjoying myself too much. I'm so grateful this book has given us even more opportunities for deep, reflective conversations.

Alexa, Jess, Erica, Marc, and Jordana, you saved my butt. Thank you all for jumping in at various moments when I was freaking out and needed your keen eyes and gift for words to make me look better.

All of the people who reacted positively when I shared this idea with you over the years; thank you for keeping this idea alive in my brain and making me eager to get it out into the world.

Megan McNally, Lindsey TH Jackson, Lauren Broomhall, Jerry Won, Chris Lee, Erin Keam, Monica Kang, Riah Gonzalez, Matt Zinman, Priyanka Komala, Terry McDougall, Martin Piskoric, and Andrew Stotz. You invited me to speak about my book with your audiences while I was still in the process of writing it. Because you gave me the chance to speak and test my thoughts out loud, I was able to refine and find new ways of communicating what I wanted to communicate. Thank you so much for your early excitement about this book and for allowing me the privilege of using your platform.

Saleema and Catalina. It was incredibly fortunate timing that I collaborated with you all when I did. My book journey would have been far less smooth and colorful without you. Thank you for your expert guidance and candidly sharing with me your own experiences.

Abbie, thank you so much for doing double duty this past year and helping me build support for this book.

The Creator Institute and New Degree Press, just *wow*. The level of support and learning I received from you is immense. Eric Koester, Brian Bies, Linda Berardelli, Benay Stein, Haley Newlin, Morgan Rohde, Amanda Brown, and more. You all made writing a book seem just so...*possible*. You not only demystified writing and publishing, but you were rocks throughout, offering an unimaginable level of access and support. Working with you all made the writing process anything but solitary. I can only hope future first-time authors find you. I would not have without the good fortune of meeting Jyoti Jani Patel.

There is no way this book would have been possible without the people who agreed to share their stories with me. Whenever I was asked what type of person or story I was looking for, my response was always, "I want to talk with people who are willing to be self-reflective and vulnerable about something they have quit." I found that in spades and my only regret is that I could not include every person's story. You all not only validated my hunch that I wasn't the only one out there with a counterintuitive take on quitting, but you also opened my eyes to a deeper level of understanding on the subject. I applaud you for your courage and vulnerability and thank you for letting me tell your story to inspire others.

Nikka, my monster. You are a joy machine.

My parents, you are the primordial ooze from which all this has evolved. Any privilege I've had to quit and iterate on my life has been because of you. I would never have learned the lessons in this book without you. Thank you, thank you, thank you, a million times thank you.

Publishing this book required a lot of support from my community even before it went to print. Thank you to all of you who preordered copies, gifted copies, shared my promotions, and joined my Author Community just to see my dream realized. You are amazing and I don't deserve you. As promised, you are mentioned below (listed in alphabetical order by first name).

THANK YOU!

Abbie Gobeli	Andrew Ohm
Abby Bass	Angela Stallbaumer
Abigail Fu	Angie Morales
Adrienne Embery-Good	Anika Anand
Alexa Peters	Anuj and Kruti
Amanda Fine	Aphrodite Bouikidis
Amanda Ungco	Arnobio Morelix
Amee Patel	Aseem Chipalkatti
Amit Bawa	Aude Broos
Amit Kohli	Baily Hancock
Amy Berman	Ben Grossman-Kahn
Andrew G. Farrand	Beth Ryan

Beth Schill

Brett Spiegel

Brittany Do

Cara Gouldey

Carlton Willey

Catherine Bender

Chandra Luczak

Charles Lipper

Charles St Charles

Chastity Butterfield

Chris Lin

Christina Cantlin Saran

Clay Andrews

Colin Nisbet

Dana Gassman

Dana Malone

Dashi Singham

Dawn Foster

Derek Law

Douglas Scherer

Elizabeth Biermann de Lancie

Ellie Anne Klein

Emily Bollen

Emily Hopkins

Eric Koester

Eric Rasmussen

Erica McIntyre

Erick Acuna

Erika Backberg

Erin Farr

Erin Keam

Esther Armstrong

Eva Lewis

Felicia Barnes

Gabby Arens & Jess Lampe

Geoff Corey

Gopa, Praveen, Anubhav, and Aakriti Kumar

Graeme Crawford

Gregg DeMammos

Harry Kacak

Heather Marie Vitale

Hema Chand

Hollie Hinton

Holly Chasan-Young

Holly Krejci

Ilin Misaras

Irene Nexica

Iris Magid

Ivy Kwong

J.J. Jackson

Jacqueline Key

Jay Gerhart

Jeffrey Bollen

Jeffrey Harry

Jeffrey Le

Jessica Day

Jessica Lee

Jessica Simon

John Carroll

Jonathan Chesebro

Joy Martinez

Judy Damschroder

Juliana Cardona Mejia

Jyoti Patel

Kaelan Sullivan

Karl Thomas Jonsson

Katherine Ryan

Kathleen Holmes

Katie Watkins

Katrina Cobb

Kay Howard

Keenan Murphy

Kelly Anderson

Kelly Razek

Ketaki Chand

Kevin McVey

Kourtney Pompi

Kushaan Shah

Kusum Gaind

Lauren Broomall

Leah Crider

Leah Kyaio

Leslie Pierson

Lisa Fain

Lisa Morales

Lynn Bulan

Maggie Greene

Marc Engel

Mary Lauran C Hall

Matt Berman

Matt Meeks

Matt Winterhalter

Meco Sparks

Meegan Roberts

Meena Rishi

Megan McNally

Melissa Chevalier

Melissa Daley

Melissa Topscher

Meredith T White

Meredith White

Mete Yurtsever

Mia Iseman

Michael Cowden

Michelle Heath

Michelle MacKenzie

Mike Kumar

Monjula Appaya

Morgan and Brendon Gideon

Murphy McHugh

Neha and Saurabh Nayyar

Nicole McKinney

Nicole Ritterstein

Noopur Shukla

Nutan and Ashni Behal

Panatda Inthala

Pavithra Tripuraneni

Philip R. Brooks

Poonam Mehta

Praveen K and Varsha Malhotra

Priyanka Rao

Rachael Paz

Rajan and Suman Behal

Rajiv Satyal

Rakesh and Archana Anand

Rakhi Mehra

Rebekah Bastian

Rohini Gandhi

Ryann Hoffman

Sabahat Chaudhary

Saleema Vellani

Sam Bonar

Samantha Hoar

Samra Akhtar

Sandra Kim

Sara Grippen

Sarah Filman

Sarah Mock

Seema Chandra

Seth Blinder

Shamila Behal

Sharon Peterson

Shaun Mathew

Shelley McIntyre

Stephanie Thum

Tavaner Sullivan

Terri Eccles

Tiffany Manchester

Varshini Balaji

Vivek Mehra and Neena Gupta

Will Bachman

Works Cited

Introduction

Novak, Matt. "The Untold Story of Napoleon Hill, The Greatest Self-Help Scammer of All Time," *Gizmodo*, December 6, 2016. https://paleofuture.gizmodo.com/the-untold-story-of-napoleon-hill-the-greatest-self-he-1789385645.

I Quit a Life of Thugs & Drugs

The Road to Wellbriety: In The Native American Way's Amazon page. Accessed February 23, 2021. https://www.amazon.com/Red-Road-Wellbriety-Native-American/dp/0971990409.

I Quit the Circus

Lee Iverson, Jonathan. "Christina Cantlin is Grounded...For Now." *HuffPo*, March 16, 2016. https://www.huffpost.com/entry/christina-cantlin-is-grou_b_9473282.

I Quit the Mormon Church

de Beauvoir, Simone. *Memoirs of a Dutiful Daughter.* New York: Harper Perennial Modern Classics, 2005).

I Quit Being a "Good Little Black Girl"

Lumet, Sidney, dir. Network. 1987; Metro-Goldwyn-Mayer (MGM).

I Quit My Mom

Meliora, Cassandra. "The People v. Cassandra Meliora." Performed live on November 21, 2019. The People's Improv Theater. Solocom 2019.

I Quit My Best Friend of Ten Years

Gervais, Ricky and Merchant, Stephen, dirs. *The Office (UK).* Series 2, episode 6, "Interview." Aired November 4, 2002, on BBC.

I Quit My Marriage

Singer, Brian, dir. *The Usual Suspects.* 1995; Gramercy Pictures.